JAMES MONROE

JAMES MONROE

Charles Wetzel

CHELSEA HOUSE PUBLISHERS
NEW YORK
PHILADELPHIA

Monroe

On the cover: *James Monroe* by Gilbert Stewart; National Gallery of Art, Washington; Ailsa Mellon Bruce Fund (detail).

Chelsea House Publishers
EDITOR-IN-CHIEF: Nancy Toff
EXECUTIVE EDITOR: Remmel T. Nunn
MANAGING EDITOR: Karyn Gullen Browne
COPY CHIEF: Juliann Barbato
PICTURE EDITOR: Adrian G. Allen
ART DIRECTOR: Maria Epes
MANUFACTURING MANAGER: Gerald Levine

World Leaders—Past & Present
SENIOR EDITOR: John W. Selfridge

Staff for JAMES MONROE
ASSISTANT EDITOR: Terrance Dolan
DEPUTY COPY CHIEF: Ellen Scordato
EDITORIAL ASSISTANT: Heather Lewis
PICTURE RESEARCHER: Joan Beard
ASSISTANT ART DIRECTOR: Laurie Jewell
DESIGNER: David Murray
PRODUCTION COORDINATOR: Joseph Romano

First Printing

1 3 5 7 9 8 6 4 2

Library of Congress Cataloging-in-Publication Data

Wetzel, Charles.
  James Monroe / Charles Wetzel.
  p.   cm.—(World leaders past & present)
  Bibliography: p.
  Includes index.
  Summary: The life and career of the fifth president, whose Monroe Doctrine proclaimed opposition to further European control in the Western Hemisphere.
  ISBN 1-55546-817-9
      0-7910-0700-6 (pbk.)
  1. Monroe, James, 1758–1831—Juvenile literature.
2. Presidents—United States—Biography—Juvenile literature.
[1. Monroe, James, 1758–1831. 2. Presidents.] I. Title. II. Series.
E372.W48   1989
973.5'4'0924—dc19   88-34372
[B]   CIP
[92]   AC

Contents

John Adams
John Quincy Adams
Konrad Adenauer
Alexander the Great
Salvador Allende
Marc Antony
Corazon Aquino
Yasir Arafat
King Arthur
Hafez al-Assad
Kemal Atatürk
Attila
Clement Attlee
Augustus Caesar
Menachem Begin
David Ben-Gurion
Otto von Bismarck
Léon Blum
Simon Bolívar
Cesare Borgia
Willy Brandt
Leonid Brezhnev
Julius Caesar
John Calvin
Jimmy Carter
Fidel Castro
Catherine the Great
Charlemagne
Chiang Kai-Shek
Winston Churchill
Georges Clemenceau
Cleopatra
Constantine the Great
Hernán Cortés
Oliver Cromwell
Georges-Jacques Danton
Jefferson Davis
Moshe Dayan
Charles de Gaulle
Eamon De Valera
Eugene Debs
Deng Xiaoping
Benjamin Disraeli
Alexander Dubček
François & Jean-Claude Duvalier
Dwight Eisenhower
Eleanor of Aquitaine
Elizabeth I
Faisal
Ferdinand & Isabella
Francisco Franco
Benjamin Franklin

Frederick the Great
Indira Gandhi
Mohandas Gandhi
Giuseppe Garibaldi
Amin & Bashir Gemayel
Genghis Khan
William Gladstone
Mikhail Gorbachev
Ulysses S. Grant
Ernesto "Che" Guevara
Tenzin Gyatso
Alexander Hamilton
Dag Hammarskjöld
Henry VIII
Henry of Navarre
Paul von Hindenburg
Hirohito
Adolf Hitler
Ho Chi Minh
King Hussein
Ivan the Terrible
Andrew Jackson
James I
Wojciech Jaruzelski
Thomas Jefferson
Joan of Arc
Pope John XXIII
Pope John Paul II
Lyndon Johnson
Benito Juárez
John Kennedy
Robert Kennedy
Jomo Kenyatta
Ayatollah Khomeini
Nikita Khrushchev
Kim Il Sung
Martin Luther King, Jr.
Henry Kissinger
Kublai Khan
Lafayette
Robert E. Lee
Vladimir Lenin
Abraham Lincoln
David Lloyd George
Louis XIV
Martin Luther
Judas Maccabeus
James Madison
Nelson & Winnie Mandela
Mao Zedong
Ferdinand Marcos
George Marshall

Mary, Queen of Scots
Tomáš Masaryk
Golda Meir
Klemens von Metternich
James Monroe
Hosni Mubarak
Robert Mugabe
Benito Mussolini
Napoléon Bonaparte
Gamal Abdel Nasser
Jawaharlal Nehru
Nero
Nicholas II
Richard Nixon
Kwame Nkrumah
Daniel Ortega
Mohammed Reza Pahlavi
Thomas Paine
Charles Stewart Parnell
Pericles
Juan Perón
Peter the Great
Pol Pot
Muammar el-Qaddafi
Ronald Reagan
Cardinal Richelieu
Maximilien Robespierre
Eleanor Roosevelt
Franklin Roosevelt
Theodore Roosevelt
Anwar Sadat
Haile Selassie
Prince Sihanouk
Jan Smuts
Joseph Stalin
Sukarno
Sun Yat-sen
Tamerlane
Mother Teresa
Margaret Thatcher
Josip Broz Tito
Toussaint L'Ouverture
Leon Trotsky
Pierre Trudeau
Harry Truman
Queen Victoria
Lech Walesa
George Washington
Chaim Weizmann
Woodrow Wilson
Xerxes
Emiliano Zapata
Zhou Enlai

CHELSEA HOUSE PUBLISHERS

ON LEADERSHIP

Arthur M. Schlesinger, jr.

LEADERSHIP, it may be said, is really what makes the world go round. Love no doubt smooths the passage; but love is a private transaction between consenting adults. Leadership is a public transaction with history. The idea of leadership affirms the capacity of individuals to move, inspire, and mobilize masses of people so that they act together in pursuit of an end. Sometimes leadership serves good purposes, sometimes bad; but whether the end is benign or evil, great leaders are those men and women who leave their personal stamp on history.

Now, the very concept of leadership implies the proposition that individuals can make a difference. This proposition has never been universally accepted. From classical times to the present day, eminent thinkers have regarded individuals as no more than the agents and pawns of larger forces, whether the gods and goddesses of the ancient world or, in the modern era, race, class, nation, the dialectic, the will of the people, the spirit of the times, history itself. Against such forces, the individual dwindles into insignificance.

So contends the thesis of historical determinism. Tolstoy's great novel *War and Peace* offers a famous statement of the case. Why, Tolstoy asked, did millions of men in the Napoleonic Wars, denying their human feelings and their common sense, move back and forth across Europe slaughtering their fellows? "The war," Tolstoy answered, "was bound to happen simply because it was bound to happen." All prior history predetermined it. As for leaders, they, Tolstoy said, "are but the labels that serve to give a name to an end and, like labels, they have the least possible connection with the event." The greater the leader, "the more conspicuous the inevitability and the predestination of every act he commits." The leader, said Tolstoy, is "the slave of history."

Determinism takes many forms. Marxism is the determinism of class. Nazism the determinism of race. But the idea of men and women as the slaves of history runs athwart the deepest human instincts. Rigid determinism abolishes the idea of human freedom—

the assumption of free choice that underlies every move we make, every word we speak, every thought we think. It abolishes the idea of human responsibility, since it is manifestly unfair to reward or punish people for actions that are by definition beyond their control. No one can live consistently by any deterministic creed. The Marxist states prove this themselves by their extreme susceptibility to the cult of leadership.

More than that, history refutes the idea that individuals make no difference. In December 1931 a British politician crossing Park Avenue in New York City between 76th and 77th Streets around 10:30 P.M. looked in the wrong direction and was knocked down by an automobile—a moment, he later recalled, of a man aghast, a world aglare: "I do not understand why I was not broken like an eggshell or squashed like a gooseberry." Fourteen months later an American politician, sitting in an open car in Miami, Florida, was fired on by an assassin; the man beside him was hit. Those who believe that individuals make no difference to history might well ponder whether the next two decades would have been the same had Mario Constasino's car killed Winston Churchill in 1931 and Giuseppe Zangara's bullet killed Franklin Roosevelt in 1933. Suppose, in addition, that Adolf Hitler had been killed in the street fighting during the Munich *Putsch* of 1923 and that Lenin had died of typhus during World War I. What would the 20th century be like now?

For better or for worse, individuals do make a difference. "The notion that a people can run itself and its affairs anonymously," wrote the philosopher William James, "is now well known to be the silliest of absurdities. Mankind does nothing save through initiatives on the part of inventors, great or small, and imitation by the rest of us—these are the sole factors in human progress. Individuals of genius show the way, and set the patterns, which common people then adopt and follow."

Leadership, James suggests, means leadership in thought as well as in action. In the long run, leaders in thought may well make the greater difference to the world. But, as Woodrow Wilson once said, "Those only are leaders of men, in the general eye, who lead in action. . . . It is at their hands that new thought gets its translation into the crude language of deeds." Leaders in thought often invent in solitude and obscurity, leaving to later generations the tasks of imitation. Leaders in action—the leaders portrayed in this series—have to be effective in their own time.

And they cannot be effective by themselves. They must act in response to the rhythms of their age. Their genius must be adapted, in a phrase of William James's, "to the receptivities of the moment." Leaders are useless without followers. "There goes the mob," said the French politician hearing a clamor in the streets. "I am their leader. I must follow them." Great leaders turn the inchoate emotions of the mob to purposes of their own. They seize on the opportunities of their time, the hopes, fears, frustrations, crises, potentialities. They succeed when events have prepared the way for them, when the community is awaiting to be aroused, when they can provide the clarifying and organizing ideas. Leadership ignites the circuit between the individual and the mass and thereby alters history.

It may alter history for better or for worse. Leaders have been responsible for the most extravagant follies and most monstrous crimes that have beset suffering humanity. They have also been vital in such gains as humanity has made in individual freedom, religious and racial tolerance, social justice, and respect for human rights.

There is no sure way to tell in advance who is going to lead for good and who for evil. But a glance at the gallery of men and women in *World Leaders—Past and Present* suggests some useful tests.

One test is this: Do leaders lead by force or by persuasion? By command or by consent? Through most of history leadership was exercised by the divine right of authority. The duty of followers was to defer and to obey. "Theirs not to reason why / Theirs but to do and die." On occasion, as with the so-called enlightened despots of the 18th century in Europe, absolutist leadership was animated by humane purposes. More often, absolutism nourished the passion for domination, land, gold, and conquest and resulted in tyranny.

The great revolution of modern times has been the revolution of equality. The idea that all people should be equal in their legal condition has undermined the old structure of authority, hierarchy, and deference. The revolution of equality has had two contrary effects on the nature of leadership. For equality, as Alexis de Tocqueville pointed out in his great study *Democracy in America*, might mean equality in servitude as well as equality in freedom.

"I know of only two methods of establishing equality in the political world," Tocqueville wrote. "Rights must be given to every citizen, or none at all to anyone . . . save one, who is the master of all." There was no middle ground "between the sovereignty of all and the absolute power of one man." In his astonishing prediction of 20th-century totalitarian dictatorship, Tocqueville explained how the revolution of equality could lead to the *"Führerprinzip"* and more terrible absolutism than the world had ever known.

But when rights are given to every citizen and the sovereignty of all is established, the problem of leadership takes a new form, becomes more exacting than ever before. It is easy to issue commands and enforce them by the rope and the stake, the concentration camp and the *gulag*. It is much harder to use argument and achievement to overcome opposition and win consent. The Founding Fathers of the United States understood the difficulty. They believed that history had given them the opportunity to decide, as Alexander Hamilton wrote in the first Federalist Paper, whether men are indeed capable of basing government on "reflection and choice, or whether they are forever destined to depend . . . on accident and force."

Government by reflection and choice called for a new style of leadership and a new quality of followership. It required leaders to be responsive to popular concerns, and it required followers to be active and informed participants in the process. Democracy does not eliminate emotion from politics; sometimes it fosters demagoguery; but it is confident that, as the greatest of democratic leaders put it, you cannot fool all of the people all of the time. It measures leadership by results and retires those who overreach or falter or fail.

It is true that in the long run despots are measured by results too. But they can postpone the day of judgment, sometimes indefinitely, and in the meantime they can do infinite harm. It is also true that democracy is no guarantee of virtue and intelligence in government, for the voice of the people is not necessarily the voice of God. But democracy, by assuring the right of opposition, offers built-in resistance to the evils inherent in absolutism. As the theologian Reinhold Niebuhr summed it up, "Man's capacity for justice makes democracy possible, but man's inclination to injustice makes democracy necessary."

A second test for leadership is the end for which power is sought. When leaders have as their goal the supremacy of a master race or the promotion of totalitarian revolution or the acquisition and exploitation of colonies or the protection of greed and privilege or the preservation of personal power, it is likely that their leadership will do little to advance the cause of humanity. When their goal is the abolition of slavery, the liberation of women, the enlargement of opportunity for the poor and powerless, the extension of equal rights to racial minorities, the defense of the freedoms of expression and opposition, it is likely that their leadership will increase the sum of human liberty and welfare.

Leaders have done great harm to the world. They have also conferred great benefits. You will find both sorts in this series. Even "good" leaders must be regarded with a certain wariness. Leaders are not demigods; they put on their trousers one leg after another just like ordinary mortals. No leader is infallible, and every leader needs to be reminded of this at regular intervals. Irreverence irritates leaders but is their salvation. Unquestioning submission corrupts leaders and demeans followers. Making a cult of a leader is always a mistake. Fortunately hero worship generates its own antidote. "Every hero," said Emerson, "becomes a bore at last."

The signal benefit the great leaders confer is to embolden the rest of us to live according to our own best selves, to be active, insistent, and resolute in affirming our own sense of things. For great leaders attest to the reality of human freedom against the supposed inevitabilities of history. And they attest to the wisdom and power that may lie within the most unlikely of us, which is why Abraham Lincoln remains the supreme example of great leadership. A great leader, said Emerson, exhibits new possibilities to all humanity. "We feed on genius. . . . Great men exist that there may be greater men."

Great leaders, in short, justify themselves by emancipating and empowering their followers. So humanity struggles to master its destiny, remembering with Alexis de Tocqueville: "It is true that around every man a fatal circle is traced beyond which he cannot pass; but within the wide verge of that circle he is powerful and free; as it is with man, so with communities."

1

In Battle Born

The 6-foot-tall, rawboned 18-year-old lieutenant from Virginia, who had quit college to fight in America's War of Independence, struggled forward through deep drifts of snow. The small company of advance guard that James Monroe had volunteered to join had come ashore in New Jersey from the ice-choked Delaware River, its waters flecked with the late glimmerings of winter dusk. On the Pennsylvania shore General George Washington and the tattered remnant of his Continental Army, having retreated through New Jersey only a few weeks earlier, waited to cross at a later moment. Captain William Washington, Monroe's senior officer and a relative of the general's, had as his mission that Christmas night in 1776 to prevent any communication between Trenton and the British to the north so that Colonel Johann Gottlieb Rall's Hessian soldiers would be isolated in their Trenton outpost and at the mercy of a surprise attack.

[James Monroe was an] enthusiastic eighteen-year-old recruit who was . . . passionately caught up by the fervor of the revolutionary cause.
—HARRY AMMON
Monroe biographer

James Monroe first demonstrated his leadership ability during the American Revolution. By the age of 18 he had risen to the rank of major in General George Washington's Continental Army. After distinguishing himself in battle, Monroe went on to play a major role in the establishment of the United States as the premier power in the Western Hemisphere.

WASHINGTON CROSSING TE DELAWARE
BOATS MANNE BY MARBLEHEA
FISHRMEN

GEN. CLOVERS REG.

In this primitive painting, George Washington stands beside the American flag in the center as his troops cross the icy Delaware River on Christmas night, 1776. The young lieutenant Monroe was among the 2,400 men who braved the bitter cold that night in order to launch a surprise attack on the British outpost at Trenton, New Jersey.

A mile and a half inland Captain Washington's men reached their objective, an intersection of the Trenton-Princeton pike. A northeast wind howled over the drifts, hurling sleety snow through the air, making conversation virtually impossible. The soldiers set up their roadblock and, as hours passed, took a number of prisoners who might otherwise have spread word that American troops had returned to New Jersey. Such information would surely have alarmed General William Howe, commander of His Majesty George III's British forces in North America. Confident that the Americans would not attack in such bad winter weather, Howe had dispersed his men in several New Jersey towns and was certain that he had already crushed the American "rebellion."

Toward dawn General Washington and his men, steering boats they had collected during their earlier retreat across the river, followed Captain Washington's route. When the general's force arrived, Monroe and his comrades fell in with the larger army as it curved south toward Trenton. They soon exchanged shots with Hessian pickets, and on December 26, the Battle of Trenton began.

In the developing conflict, 26-year-old Colonel Henry Knox, a rotund Boston ex-bookseller in charge of General Washington's cannon, brought his artillery to bear, raking the streets of the town with shot that scattered Rall's still half-drowsing troops as they fell out of their barracks. Assisting Knox was another young college dropout Monroe's age, Alexander Hamilton, a recent immigrant from the West Indies.

Rall's artillerymen tried desperately to get their own guns into action, galloping the horse-drawn caissons toward the front lines, but Knox's withering fire discouraged them, and one by one they abandoned their efforts. To prevent the Hessians mounting their cannon, Captain Washington and Monroe led a charge to seize the enemy guns. The Hessians focused their aim on the exposed Americans, and William Washington fell, his hands pierced by musket shot. Monroe continued to lead the charge, but within moments an enemy ball struck him as well, tearing through his shoulder to sever an artery. Both men were quickly carried off the battlefield.

Without immediate attention, Monroe would have bled to death on the spot, but a surgeon who, providentially, had voluntarily attached himself to Captain Washington's outfit before the battle hastened to stem the flow of blood. The doctors aiding the American army that day could not know that they served the future first president of the United States and key members of his administration. As for the young Virginia lieutenant whose life was saved, they had no reason to imagine that after serving the fledgling republic in many important positions, he would become the fifth president of the United States and promulgate one of the most famous foreign policy declarations in American history — the Monroe Doctrine.

James Monroe was born on April 28, 1758, in Westmoreland County, Virginia, the county that had already been birthplace to two men who would precede him as president, George Washington and James Madison. The largest and oldest of the colonies that would form the original United States,

The British outpost at Trenton was manned primarily by Hessian grenadiers such as the one pictured here. Although the Hessians — German mercenaries employed by the Crown — were battle-hardened veterans, they were taken entirely by surprise during the pre-dawn hours of December 26. Nine hundred and eighteen Hessians were captured; 30 were killed.

The portly Colonel Henry Knox, Washington's artillery commander, stands before one of the cannons that enabled the American force to rout the Hessians at Trenton. Knox went on to succeed Washington as commander of the Continental Army and eventually became U.S. secretary of war.

Virginia held great prominence, dictated by its size and history and by the political and intellectual brilliance of many of its foremost citizens. Like leaders in other parts of America, distinguished Virginians turned to men of their own class when they thought in terms of friendships and political offices. Fortunately for James Monroe's future, his father, Spence Monroe, though not one of the Old Dominion's wealthiest citizens, had property sufficient to qualify him as a respectable, though minor, landed gentleman. Monroe's mother, Elizabeth Jones, the daughter of a Welsh immigrant, inherited additional property in King George County, which helped increase the Monroe family's standing.

The Monroe lineage was a worthy one by Virginia standards. According to family legend, Andrew Monroe, a Scottish highlander, had been an officer in King Charles I's army in 1648, when it fought Oliver Cromwell's Puritan forces in the Battle of Preston. With Charles's subsequent defeat and execution, Andrew Monroe had emigrated to the Chesapeake Bay region and settled in Virginia. As descendants of this founder of one of the "Cavalier" families — the distinguished royalist refugees from Charles I's service — the Monroes enjoyed a special status in Virginia society.

James Monroe's credentials further improved because his wealthy uncle on his mother's side, Judge Joseph Jones, sat firmly with the colony's ruling elite. Trained in the law in England, a noted member of the Virginia House of Burgesses (the colony's legislative assembly), a man who would distinguish himself in the revolutionary cause, represent Virginia in the Continental Congress, and end his life as a state supreme court justice, Jones would earn much more space in the autobiography James Monroe wrote late in life than would James's own father.

The birthplace of James Monroe, in Westmoreland County, Virginia. Revolutionary ideas flourished in the fertile Virginia countryside; the original colony yielded many of the founders of the United States of America, including George Washington, James Madison, Thomas Jefferson, and Patrick Henry.

When Spence Monroe died in 1774, Judge Jones arranged for James to be enrolled at William and Mary College, the first of the Monroes to be afforded that opportunity. James, who had begun his formal education at age 11 at the best local school available to him, entered the college with such a mastery of Latin and mathematics that he was placed in the upper division.

Having grown up in the rural tidewater with a love for the land, for farming, and for such country pleasures as riding and hunting (which remained with him throughout his life), James Monroe found Williamsburg, Virginia's capital and site of the college, delightful and stimulating. In the summer of 1774, however, the political atmosphere was perhaps a bit too stimulating for Monroe to concentrate on his studies. The House of Burgesses, its activities suspended by Virginia's royal governor, Lord Dunmore, because of its radical sympathies with rebellious colonists, met illegally in the Raleigh Tavern to continue "governing." When Dunmore impounded the town's gunpowder to deprive the radicals of potential arms, his act incited Patrick Henry,

William and Mary College, in Williamsburg, Virginia, as it looked in the summer of 1774, when 16-year-old James Monroe enrolled there. Like many of the larger colonial towns of that period, Williamsburg was a hotbed of revolutionary agitation and intrigue.

"There is a time to fight, and that time has now come!" proclaimed fiery colonial orator Patrick Henry in April 1775. Monroe was one of the many citizens of Virginia to heed Henry's inflammatory words and take up arms against the British Crown.

a rebel whose oratory would fire the country, to march on Williamsburg with a following of irate colonists to persuade Dunmore to change his mind. As these events unfolded and the relationship between the British and the American colonials rapidly deteriorated, Monroe and some of his fellow students armed themselves to support the American cause, defying the college administration's demand that they surrender their weapons. On April 19, 1775, fighting between British regulars and American rebels at Lexington and Concord in Massachusetts signaled the start of the American Revolution. In Williamsburg on June 24, Monroe joined in an attack on the governor's palace to seize arms stored there. In the spring of 1776, he quit school to enlist in the Third Virginia Infantry and soon became a lieutenant.

In August the Third Virginia was ordered north to New York City to swell the ranks of General George Washington's Continental Army. By the time they arrived, British troops had driven the Americans from their positions on York Island (now Long Island). Monroe first saw action on Manhattan, sallying from the Harlem Heights against an approaching British force. Of three young officers sent into the engagement, he alone survived, so that when spared at Trenton his life seemed twice charmed.

After the Harlem incident, Monroe came through a second trial of fire at White Plains, where George Washington struggled fruitlessly to hold New York City and its environs. Monroe next took part in the retreat of some 3,000 soldiers across the Hudson River and through New Jersey on tortuous roads that led finally to the Delaware. Monroe especially admired George Washington's courage and determination in retreat, his refusal to give up, his constant presence at the rear to face the pursuing enemy. When Monroe later faced allegations of failing in his efforts as an American diplomat, he remembered Washington as a model for surviving adversity.

George Washington, on his familiar white steed, and the Marquis de Lafayette, the young French officer who inspired American troops throughout the revolutionary war, survey the situation at the Battle of Monmouth, New Jersey, in this colonial-era painting. France officially aligned itself with the United States against England on February 6, 1778.

Like many young men of his time, Monroe hoped to launch a career through advancement in the army's officer corps. He soon discovered, however, that Washington had a gentleman's scruples about the niceties of promotion; older men with longer service were given preferment. Monroe's case was doubly doomed because Washington had no desire to rouse political and military opposition by seeming to give special rewards to fellow Virginians.

Monroe took three months to recover from the wound he received at Trenton. Knowing Washington's practice regarding promotions, Monroe left the Continental Army to undertake a trip to Virginia to try to raise a volunteer force under his personal leadership and thus, perhaps, get a promotion via the back door. Undaunted by his failure to do so, he rejoined the troops in the North as a volunteer aide-de-camp (with the rank of major) to one of Washington's subordinates, General William Alexander. Alexander, who was born in America, held title to a Scottish earldom and was known as Lord Stirling. Monroe's new position enabled him to begin or renew friendships with a number of men destined to be important in his future. These included Hamilton; John Marshall of Virginia, who had been a schoolmate of Monroe's at the small academy he had attended before William and Mary and was now Stirling's judge advocate; Aaron Burr, a colonel in Lord Stirling's brigade; and the young, enthusiastic Marquis de Lafayette, a fervent supporter of the American Revolution and the most renowned of the French volunteers who fought for its cause.

Traveling with Stirling in Washington's army, Monroe came under fire at both Brandywine and Germantown, battles Washington engaged in hoping to prevent the British occupation of Philadelphia, then America's capital. In 1777–78, Monroe spent a bitter winter at Valley Forge learning yet another lesson in endurance with a dejected army whose spirit was at its lowest point. When the new British commander, General George Clinton, abandoned Philadelphia and drew back toward New York City in 1778, Monroe fought in his last major engagement of the war, the Battle of Monmouth in

A battered, demoralized, and ill-equipped Continental army bivouacked for the winter of 1777–78 at Valley Forge, Pennsylvania, where conditions were brutal. It is believed that at least 3,000 men died at Valley Forge from exposure to the bitter elements and a lack of necessary supplies. Monroe was one of those who survived the deadly winter.

LIBERTY
TREE

A cartoon from a London
newspaper depicts the situation in Boston during the
British blockade of Boston
Harbor prior to the outbreak
of the Revolution. The citizens of Boston are depicted
as starving, caged criminals
eating raw fish offered by fellow colonists.

New Jersey. Although the battle was not a true victory for the Americans — the British escaped intact
— the Americans were encouraged that Washington's army finally proved itself a strong, disciplined
opponent.

At the end of the year Monroe left Stirling's service. Still impatient to have a command of his own,
he headed south to Virginia a second time, hoping
again to raise his own force, only to suffer another
disappointment. His plan to join the state militia
also fell through, and he was unsure of which way
to turn when, in 1780, he met Virginia's wartime
governor, Thomas Jefferson, who took a liking to
the young veteran. Thus began the most significant
friendship of Monroe's life.

Already renowned as the author of the Declaration

of Independence, Jefferson, 15 years his young friend's senior, assumed the role of Monroe's mentor. The governor encouraged Monroe to study law and prepare for a political career. Given a choice between reading the law under the tutelage of the distinguished George Wythe, the most famous legal scholar of the age and Jefferson's former teacher, or with Jefferson himself, Monroe chose Jefferson, the man more likely to be politically useful in the future. When Jefferson moved to Richmond, the new capital of Virginia, Monroe followed.

In 1782, with the war all but over and Washington's victorious army quietly encamped on the Hudson River awaiting the conclusion of peace negotiations, Monroe formally entered politics. He was elected to his uncle's seat in the Virginia House of Delegates when Judge Jones became a member of the Virginian delegation to the Continental Congress. Within a short time, Monroe's legislative colleagues arranged for him to sit on the Governor's Council, a position with little power but immense prestige for a newcomer. The council, a remnant from the royal government, consisted of eight councillors and the state governor. It acted as the executive power of the state. Here Monroe began to reveal his promise not as a flashy meteor in the political sky or as a brilliant scholar-statesman in the Jefferson mold but as a hardworking, practical politician who made solid, well-reasoned judgments. In an age when principles formed the basis of political argumentation, Monroe, not the equal of some others in bookish erudition, made up for it in honesty and good sense.

As a member of the council, one of the areas Monroe took a keen interest in was the development of the West (the region west of the Allegheny Mountains). He began a correspondence with George Rogers Clark, who was fighting Indians in that area, to learn more about the region. After a year, Monroe's performance as a councillor was solid enough to land him an even more important position — delegate to the Continental Congress. By 1783, Monroe had already emerged as a significant patriot-leader. It was a role he would assume for the remainder of his days.

Thomas Jefferson, drafting the Declaration of Independence by candlelight. Monroe first met Jefferson in 1780 in Virginia. It was at Jefferson's prompting that Monroe returned to school after the war to prepare himself for a career in politics.

2

Minister to Revolution

At the end of 1783, Monroe left Virginia for An-
napolis, Maryland, to serve in the Congress. Since
its origin in 1774, this body had dealt with a number of matters, including protests against British
policies, the formal declaration of independence,
the conduct of the war and diplomacy, and matters
regarding wartime economic policy. It was now the
center of intense activity as it began to work out the
form and function of a new national government.
Although Monroe did not wish to see the rewards
of victory squandered by a weak government, he,
along with fellow delegate Jefferson and many others, harbored serious doubts about the extent to
which political authority could be safely centralized.
The United States had, after all, come into being
out of protest against a remote and overly powerful
government.

**James Monroe addressed the revolutionary French as-
sembly in 1794. Monroe's debut as an American diplomat was an inauspicious one; although the new French
government responded enthusiastically to his pro-
France overtures, the enthusiasm soured when it was
learned that the United States had signed a treaty with
France's archrival, Great Britain.**

One issue taken up by Congress struck a chord in Monroe — the plan for the government of the West. Congress contained many men who had extensive claims to lands west of the Appalachian Mountains and who were concerned about land policies and the extension of government and security to that area. Monroe wanted to see this frontier region first-hand, and when Congress adjourned in June 1784, he prepared for a trip west. He and Jefferson had designed the trip to better understand and plan for that region's future. Jefferson, however, was sent to France as an envoy and did not make the journey. But Monroe pushed on, and this trip, together with a second one he made in 1785, helped him to play an important part in shaping congressional policy on the region.

Monroe's 1784 tour west began in upper New York State, where he traveled with a group of state commissioners trying to assert control of Indian affairs there. During his trip, Monroe noted with dismay that the British, who still commanded many forts on U.S. soil, appeared unwilling to relinquish any control. However, Monroe was well received at Niagara, where the British commander warned the American party that its plan to travel onward to Fort Erie along an easier Canadian route would expose it to possible attack from hostile Indians. Monroe alone took his advice and went to Erie on the American side accompanied by a reliable Indian guide. But there he ended his trip when he learned that most of those who had chosen the Canadian route had been massacred.

The year 1785 proved to be a better one. Congress, which had transferred to Trenton in October 1784, relocated the following January to the more cosmopolitan New York City, dramatically improving the morale of its members. During the second session, Monroe emerged as a recognized leader and held several important committee seats. He continued to show an interest in issues affecting the West and tried to set up a committee to address the problem of the British forts in the Northwest. On a vacation in August, Monroe made his second journey west, this one destined to be far more successful.

I am of opinion that it will be for the benefit of the U.S. that the river shod. be opened . . . if we enter'd into engagements to the contrary, we separate these people,—I mean all those westd. of the mountains from the federal government & perhaps throw them into the hands . . . of a foreign power.
—JAMES MONROE
on the Jay-Gardoqui Treaty

James Madison, the brilliant Virginia politician whom Monroe had come to know during the first congressional session and whose friendship with Monroe Jefferson had been furthering, had hoped to go along, but through a mix-up he failed to meet Monroe in New York. This time Monroe journeyed via Pittsburgh into the Ohio country, then turned south toward Kentucky, finally reaching Lexington. When he returned to Congress in the fall, he was probably the best informed, most sympathetic, and most recognized spokesman the West had at that time.

After his return, Monroe proceeded to help the West in two important ways. He chaired a committee whose job it was to revise Jefferson's Land Ordinance of 1784, a plan that had detailed the structure of local government in the West and had outlined the provisions for statehood for the western territories. Monroe contributed significantly to the revised land bill, which, when it passed after Monroe had ended his three-year term in Congress in 1786, became known as the Northwest Ordinance of 1787. The Northwest Ordinance delineated the process of territorial development that would eventually lead to the creation of new states in the West.

Cumberland Gap, a high pass in the Cumberland Mountains on the border between Kentucky and Tennessee. Monroe traveled through this region in 1784 and 1785, and he was instrumental in the passing of legislation that would lead to U.S. expansion into the western territories.

Irate citizens burn U.S. secretary of foreign affairs John Jay in effigy. Americans throughout the western territories were outraged in 1787 when Jay attempted to persuade Congress to concede the Mississippi River to Spain, a move that Monroe and a number of other southern politicians successfully prevented.

Monroe's second important contribution to the West's future was his staunch opposition to the Jay-Gardoqui Treaty. John Jay, the secretary of foreign affairs, had been given approval to negotiate with Don Diego de Gardoqui, the first Spanish minister to the United States. In return for important trade concessions from Spain, Jay wanted Congress to give up its opposition to Spanish claims of total possession of the Mississippi River. What Jay was asking was that Americans living in the West be left hostages to Spanish control of the river system that was vital to their trade with the outside world. Together with other southern politicians, including Charles Pinckney of South Carolina, Monroe successfully battled the northerners who favored ratifying the Jay-Gardoqui draft treaty. Indeed, Monroe was largely responsible for preventing its ratification.

During his congressional term, Monroe showed a growing interest in the expansion of U.S. commerce. In the first session, he had tried to convince others of the necessity of amending the Articles of Confederation, the constitution the country had been operating under since the Revolution, to allow Congress to regulate trade and commerce. He had to drop his talk of amendments when he received no support from the rest of Congress. But the need to somehow revise the Articles of Confederation, which was too weak to be effective, was becoming increasingly apparent, and when a proposal was made for a convention of all the states to revise the Articles, Monroe supported it. The constitutional convention would meet in Philadelphia in 1787.

After his congressional term ended in 1786, Monroe returned reluctantly to Virginia to take up the practice of law. Monroe apparently did not really relish the vocation as such, but he needed the money. Never highly successful in his private ventures, Monroe was always concerned about sources of income. When Monroe arrived in Virginia, Judge Jones discouraged him from starting his law career in competitive Richmond and suggested he go to Fredericksburg, a smaller, less expensive town that offered greater opportunities for both professional and political advancement.

In 1787, delegates gathered in Philadelphia, Pennsylvania, for the Constitutional Convention. Although Monroe had been one of the first to call for a revision of the Articles of Confederation, he was not selected as a Virginia delegate to the convention, and he initially opposed ratification of the new Constitution.

A miniature of Elizabeth Kortright, the daughter of a Dutch merchant. Monroe first met Kortright in New York, and in 1786 they were married in Fredericksburg, Virginia. Her poise and charm would prove valuable assets to Monroe's political career.

To Fredericksburg, Monroe brought his new wife, whom he had met while serving in the Congress in New York. They were married in February 1786. Elizabeth Kortright was the daughter of a former West Indies merchant who had moved to New York City before the War for Independence. Elizabeth appeared in public with great reserve and propriety, almost aloofness, but in private she was a warm and loving companion. She was remarkably beautiful and could be very charming, which would help Monroe in his political career. By December, Monroe was firmly established as a family man when his first child, Eliza, was born. The Monroes would have another daughter, Maria Hester, and a son who died young in 1800.

Once settled in Fredericksburg, Monroe resumed his political career. In the spring of 1787 he was elected to the Virginia House of Delegates. His hope that he might be part of the state's delegation sent to the constitutional convention in Philadelphia was soon dashed, but within a year he was at the Virginia convention called to consider ratification of the new constitution drawn up in Philadelphia by Madison and others. By that time Monroe had allied himself with the strong anticentralist faction in the state legislature that opposed the new constitution. Monroe had earlier supported a strong federal government, but back in Virginia he was exposed to the views of such strong states' rights advocates as Patrick Henry, Edmund Randolph, and George Mason, not to mention his uncle, Judge Jones. After listening to them, Monroe began to fear that the new constitution concentrated too much power in the federal government. Monroe was not as radical as Henry; he did not so much want to reject the new framework as to refashion it in ways that seemed necessary to safeguard against rampant federal power. Like most of the antifederalists, Monroe opposed the lack of a bill of rights and a senate that was not based on popular election. However, he was one of the most moderate of the antifederalists and, in fact, supported several federalist stands, including a strong executive with a veto power over legislation and federal control of the state militias.

The Virginia convention, which met in June 1788, was the scene of fierce debates before it ratified the new constitution — on the assumption that amendments would be added. Monroe sat on the committee that drew up the proposed amendments. That same year, Monroe was persuaded by the antifederalists to run against James Madison for a seat in the new federal Congress. Madison defeated him, but the two friends resumed their correspondence, tactfully avoiding discussion of their differences over the Constitution.

Soon after, Jefferson, who had been in France during the constitutional convention and ratification process, returned to America, and in 1790 he supported Monroe's successful bid for the U.S. Senate. In December, Monroe arrived in Philadelphia to join the Congress. Jefferson, appointed the nation's first secretary of state that year, roomed at the same boardinghouse with Representative Madison, and these two men, who were destined to have a great effect on the country's future, invited Monroe to join them. Within a short time, Monroe assumed in the Senate, as Madison had in the House, leadership of a faction called Republican, with Jefferson as its center.

In 1788, Monroe ran against his friend and fellow Virginian James Madison — portrayed here in an engraving — for a seat in the new federal Congress. Although Monroe was defeated overwhelmingly, he continued his friendship with Madison.

U.S. secretary of the Treasury Alexander Hamilton. Upon joining Congress in 1790, Monroe quickly aligned himself with the antifederalist faction led by Jefferson and Madison. The antifederalists, who came to be known as the Republicans, opposed the policies of Federalist Hamilton, who advocated a strong central government.

Monroe shared with Jefferson, Madison, and other Republicans the firm conviction that the Federalists, formed by and around Alexander Hamilton, the new secretary of the Treasury, intended to impose a form of highly centralized or even monarchical government on the United States. This government, the Republicans believed, would serve the selfish interests of a small group of wealthy men in commerce and industry. New federal innovations, proposed tariffs to protect industrial development, a national bank owned largely by private investors, and the use of federal monies to redeem war bonds that had been bought up over the years by speculators all seemed to the Republicans to be immoral and dangerous abuses of constitutional power.

Monroe worked against Federalist measures aimed at strengthening the government's economic control over the states. Monroe also sat on a Senate committee formed in 1792 to investigate charges that Hamilton had used his cabinet position to fatten his own fortune through speculation. (Hamilton later revealed privately that the money his detractors thought was from the treasury fund, supposedly used by him for private investment, had been his own and was paid as blackmail to hush up an adulterous affair he had had.)

The two parties split over the recent revolution in France. The French, who overthrew their monarch in 1789, professed to follow the same ideals of republicanism that had driven the American colonists to revolt. Fearful of the radical French revolutionaries, several European nations, led by Great Britain, Austria, and Prussia, had joined in an anti-French coalition. France struck back belligerently; in February 1793 it declared war on Great Britain. The Republicans had supported the French Revolution. The Federalists, eager for good relations with Great Britain, were reluctant to embrace the French in their rebellion. Washington favored a policy of neutrality, hoping to avoid antagonizing either nation.

As the revolution in France went through several stages, each more radical than the last, French officials requested that Gouverneur Morris, the American minister to France and a Federalist, be recalled. In 1794, Washington, trying to subdue partisan strife over foreign policy and to quiet French fears that the United States favored Britain, sought a suitable Republican for the French post. Some Republican leaders suggested Aaron Burr, whom Washington did not trust. The president finally settled on Senator Monroe. Unfortunately, the new secretary of state, Edmund Randolph, did not explain to Monroe that the American minister to Britain, John Jay, was in the midst of negotiating a new treaty with Britain to resolve such problems as British forces on American soil and to establish better trade relations. News of the negotiations would greatly disturb the French.

French revolutionary Maximilien De Robespierre, known as "The Incorruptible," was one of the most prominent figures in the 1792 overthrow of the monarchy of Louis XVI. Robespierre, who initiated a political reign of terror, was guillotined shortly before Monroe arrived in France in July 1794.

Monroe reached Paris just days after the most radical of the revolutioinary leaders, Robespierre, had been executed by a rival faction. The new revolutionary government, called the Committee of Public Safety, distrusted the United States and delayed its reception of the new American emissary. Attempting to get around this impasse, Monroe finally managed an invitation to speak to the revolutionary leaders and, in his enthusiasm and partisan Republican sympathy for France, intimated in his speech far warmer support for the Revolution than his superiors in the Washington administration intended. Amid cheers and applause, the American and French flags (the former furnished by Monroe himself) were displayed together in a great show of U.S.-French harmony.

Monroe next proceeded to get Thomas Paine released from prison, which Gouverneur Morris had refused to do. Paine, a supporter of the American Revolution, perceived himself as a revolutionary of the world and had gone to France to serve the cause there. But he had identified with the wrong political faction at the wrong time and been jailed. Monroe not only obtained his release, but the Monroes extended the hospitality of their home to the ardent supporter of liberty. However, Paine made some injudicious remarks about President Washington that embarrassed his Virginia benefactor and would ultimately play a part in Monroe's recall from France.

Monroe's overenthusiastic speech and his involvement with Paine did him little good back in America. Secretary of State Randolph chided him for his indiscretion. In good conscience Monroe tried to convince the French authorities that John Jay's mission to Britain did not threaten French interests. But Monroe's position with the French was undermined when news arrived that late in 1794 Jay had concluded a new treaty with the British. The French were enraged at what they could only view as the cementing of a potential Anglo-American alliance against France, a clear violation of America's supposed neutrality.

Monroe, caught unaware by Jay's treaty, felt betrayed by his government. He hoped that it would be rejected in the Senate, and he tried to reassure the French on this score. But word came that the Senate had quickly ratified the treaty and Washington had signed it. Meanwhile, the new secretary of state, Timothy Pickering, was becoming increasingly angered by Monroe's failure to justify to the French the administration's position regarding Britain; rather, Monroe seemed to be posing as a spokesman for the American public in opposition to the administration, allowing his partisan alliances to overtake his duty to his government. Pickering, a stalwart Federalist, intended to have Monroe's head on a platter, and in 1796, together with Hamilton, persuaded Washington, as one of his last acts, to recall Monroe and replace him with Charles Cotesworth Pinckney, a man considered more responsive to the administration's directives.

Revolutionary-war pamphleteer Thomas Paine traveled to France in 1792 to participate in the French Revolution, but was thrown in prison by Robespierre for protesting the execution of Louis XVI. Monroe managed to secure Paine's release during his term as minister to France.

An artist's conception of the chaos and bloodshed unleashed by the French Revolution. Although the French revolutionaries were inspired by their American counterparts, an orgy of political persecution and reprisal followed the overthrow of the French monarchy.

Monroe, for all his mistakes in allowing his enthusiasm and sympathy to create a profound misunderstanding about official U.S. policy regarding France, had managed to prevent a rift from opening between the two countries. News of Monroe's recall ended that tenuous accord. The Directory, which had come to power in 1795 as the latest governing body of the Revolution, declared American ships subject to the same treatment as enemy British ships. When Pinckney arrived in December 1796 to replace Monroe, the Directory refused to receive him. The Monroes could do little but pack up and go home, albeit reluctantly. They had developed a love of French furnishings and opulence that would remain for the rest of their lives and make Monroe's ongoing financial problems doubly vexing.

When their ship docked in Philadelphia in June 1797, the Monroes must have been at least mildly surprised at their reception. The new vice-president, Thomas Jefferson, came aboard their ship. Accompanying him were two top members of the Republican party, Aaron Burr of New York and Albert Gallatin of Pennsylvania. Within days, Jefferson and a host of congressmen gave a great dinner in the capital to celebrate Monroe's return. Shortly thereafter, Monroe went to New York to attend another gala dinner, hosted by General Horatio Gates, the revolutionary war hero of the Battle of Saratoga. Republicans were determined to make Monroe's recall a focal point of protest against the Federalists, now in power under President John Adams.

No longer a public servant, Monroe returned to Virginia and to private life. He undertook to answer the many criticisms, often malicious, of his mission to France. Some were difficult to rebut, for Monroe never received a clear statement of the reasons for his "disgrace." Before leaving office, Secretary of State Pickering had made it a point to refuse to give any particulars on the matter. Federalist enemies contended, among other things, that Monroe had engaged in personal profiteering in France, that he had privately undermined the Washington administration's efforts by supplying the administration's enemies with information, and that he had harbored and encouraged critics of Washington, including Paine.

In several hundred pages of reprinted documents and text Monroe offered his *View of the Conduct of the Executive, in the Foreign Affairs of the United States.* Monroe poured out his hurts, loyalties, and ambitions in the work. As so often happened in his life, he felt himself to have been wronged and let down by others whom he had trusted. Monroe tended to feel that a personal dislike of him prompted his enemies to act against him. In truth, though he could not admit it, in France he had overstepped his instructions, believing that he understood the American situation better than his superiors did. He had not represented his government, the proper job of a diplomat, but rather his party and personal interests.

It was in France, however, that Monroe revealed a growing obsession with the idea that America's security lay in strong and positive relationships with other powers, not in neutral isolation. He had begun to adopt a vision of a United States that would assume its rightful place as one of the major nations of the world, imposing its will rather than merely trying to deal with the consequences of the wills of other nations.

> *I have been injured by the administration and I have a right to redress.*
> —JAMES MONROE
> on his recall from France

3

State and Empire

Monroe reluctantly returned to the practice of law, his struggle with debt by now chronic. But he could not give up his aspiration for a public career, made more compelling by virtue of his importance to the Republican party, which had its eyes on the upcoming national elections of 1800.

In 1799, Monroe ran as the Republican candidate for governor of Virginia, an office he won and held for three consecutive terms, the maximum time allowed. Virginia's governors, though, had little real power and no veto or ability to make appointments to state offices. The state constitution, dating from the revolutionary period of 1776, reflected fears and apprehensions about government, especially "royal" and "executive" powers. Governors had to win over the majority of the eight-member council in order to act and were largely limited to providing moral leadership and inspiration. Monroe did introduce various reforms in education and proposals for increased road construction and the improvement of jails and the state's military system. But he had

In electing Monroe governor in 1799, the Republicans had been as much concerned with the political aspects of that office as with either his vindication or his ability as an executive.
—HARRY AMMON
Monroe biographer

In New Orleans, subjects of French emperor Napoleon Bonaparte react with dismay to the news of the Louisiana Purchase. Napoleon sold the Louisiana Territory to the United States in order to finance his war against England.

scant success against conservative opponents eager to prevent any rise in taxes. His most visible contribution as governor was his activity on behalf of Republican candidates in 1800.

Monroe's gubernatorial years proved less satisfying than he expected them to be. He suffered a personal loss when his only son, born in 1799, died in 1800. In the same year, he had to deal with a yellow fever epidemic that threatened the state. One of the most important problems he faced as governor was Gabriel's uprising, the first major slave revolt of the 19th century in the United States and a precursor of the 1832 rebellion led by Nat Turner.

Gabriel, a 24-year-old slave alert to events in the world outside the plantation he worked on, believed that the ringing declarations of liberty and equality expressed in the American and French revolutions were meant for blacks as well as whites. Recently, on the island of Saint-Domingue (modern Hispaniola), a black leader named Toussaint L'Ouverture had led a successful uprising against the ruling French masters. Gabriel hoped to emulate Toussaint's feat. But on the night of the revolt, August 30, 1800, a devastating storm broke the back of the attempt, even though upward of a thousand armed slaves gathered to take part. The authorities began to round up any blacks who could be identified with the plot, beginning with Gabriel.

Monroe may have had an inkling of the rebellion in advance because he wrote to Jefferson on April 22 of a rumored uprising. The authorities were tipped off on the eve of the event, and Monroe, placing himself in command, quickly tried to mobilize the manpower needed to put down the slaves. After the revolt was suppressed, Monroe favored leniency for those who he thought deserved it. He personally interviewed Gabriel in prison, hoping to learn more about the motives of the rebels, but found the black leader unwilling to talk and resolved to die. In the end Gabriel and a number of other ringleaders were executed.

Monroe must have felt especially uncomfortable during this crisis. As a southerner and slave owner,

[Gabriel was] a fellow of courage and intellect above his rank in life.

—JOHN THOMPSON
CALLENDER

he understood perfectly the desperate need to retain absolute control over the system. The southern plantation owners felt that unwillingness or inability to meet any plot or uprising with immediate force would invite massive rebellion. Yet Monroe recognized and even sympathized with the slaves' determination not to accept their lot. Like Jefferson, Monroe had ambivalent feelings about slavery, especially when viewing it in the light of the pronouncements contained in the Declaration of Independence. Like his friend and mentor, Monroe hoped for a peaceful, gradual end to the system. Monroe would later support the efforts of the American Colonization Society, begun in 1817, to estab-

As governor of Virginia, Monroe put down Gabriel's uprising, a revolt by over 1,000 slaves. Thirty-two years later, another slave uprising would occur in Virginia, organized by Nat Turner. Turner, whose capture is depicted in this drawing, was hunted down with his comrades and hanged.

Monrovia is the capital and main port of the West African nation of Liberia. The city was named in honor of Monroe, who supported the efforts of the American Colonization Society to establish Liberia as an African homeland for freed American slaves.

lish an African homeland for free, or manumitted, American blacks. As president, he would allow agents of the society to use federal funds to lay the groundwork for Liberia, a West African country whose capital still bears his name — Monrovia. Monroe is, in fact, the only American president for whom a foreign capital is named.

After he retired from the governorship in 1801, Monroe decided that his reputation was sufficiently established to justify setting up a legal practice in Richmond. In the next two years he declined public offices and instead pursued ways to scale down his substantial indebtedness. But in January 1803 he assumed a public role once again, this time as envoy extraordinary and minister plenipotentiary to Napoleonic France. Now Monroe would be serving the man who had meant so much to him throughout his political career, Thomas Jefferson.

In 1801, Jefferson, who had defeated Adams for

the presidency in 1800, and his secretary of state, James Madison, learned that France had retrieved the vast territory known as Louisiana from Spain, to which France had ceded it in 1763. The Louisiana Territory comprised the western half of the Mississippi River basin, extending from the modern state of Louisiana north to Minnesota and west to the Rocky Mountains. Napoleon Bonaparte, the young general who had imposed his leadership on revolutionary France in a coup in 1799, was soon to declare himself emperor. Together with his foreign minister, Charles-Maurice de Talleyrand, Napoleon conceived a grand scheme to establish part of his powerful empire in the New World by using Louisiana as a food source for France's several Caribbean islands. Talleyrand saw French ownership of the territory also as a way to prevent the further westward growth of the United States; Spain was too weak to prevent American expansion.

Concerned about the French taking control of the Mississippi River and its outlet, New Orleans, Jefferson quickly dispatched the new U.S. minister to France, Robert Livingston. Livingston received instructions to seek some arrangement regarding Louisiana that would satisfy the United States. If Livingston could not prevent the transfer, he was to ask for French assistance to obtain a cession of West Florida by Spain to the United States to guarantee the American West access to the Gulf of Mexico and ocean ports. If that failed, then Livingston was to imply that the United States might ally with Great Britain in pursuit of its interests.

In 1802, preparing to turn Louisiana over to France, Spanish authorities in the New World ended the privilege extended to Americans of a duty-free deposit area at New Orleans, where goods from the United States could be off-loaded and reloaded onto oceangoing ships. This raised an alarm over the economic future of the West, and those affected blamed the French. The Federalists, looking for a popular issue, called for war. Eager to avoid a military conflict, anxious to placate the West (which was a bastion of Republicanism), and desirous of a permanent solution to the problem of western commerce, Jefferson sent Monroe as a special envoy to join Livingston. His choice signaled to westerners that the administration had their best interests at heart; Monroe's reputation as a knowledgeable pro-westerner gave a legitimacy to the administration's efforts to negotiate a settlement. Jefferson also secured from Congress a fund of $2 million for the negotiations.

Livingston had already proceeded a long way toward an agreement with France before Monroe arrived, but Monroe carried important new instructions from Jefferson. Minimally the United States wanted a part of New Orleans to call its own and free passage on the rivers that flowed southward from the United States through the Floridas into the Gulf of Mexico. If possible, Jefferson wanted all of New Orleans and a significant part of the Floridas. Monroe was told to warn the French that the

[Y]ou have made a noble bargain for yourselves and I suppose you will make the most of it.

—TALLEYRAND
French statesman, on the
Louisiana Purchase

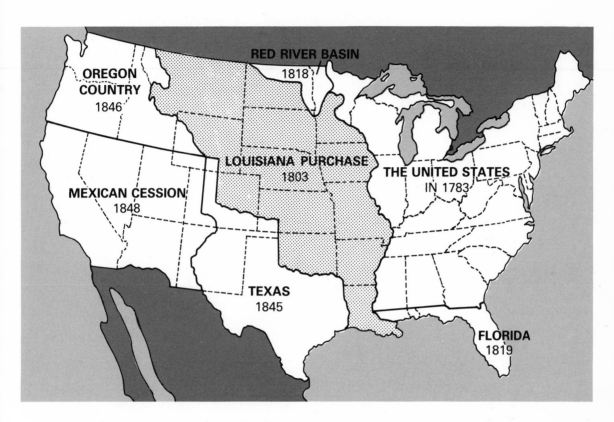

The lightly shaded area of this map represents the 828,000 square-mile Louisiana Purchase, acquired from French emperor Napoleon Bonaparte in 1803 for $15 million. U.S. minister to France Robert Livingston and special envoy Monroe made the purchase — without the approval of President Jefferson — thus doubling the size of the United States.

United States would not brook either French or British absolute control of the mouth of the Mississippi.

Before Monroe reached Paris, however, Napoleon had lost heart over his New World project. An army commanded by his brother-in-law that he had sent to reclaim Saint-Domingue had succeeded in suppressing the rebellion and killing Toussaint L'Ouverture, but then it had fallen victim to deadly fever. Napoleon's attention had shifted back to his plans for European conquest and imminent war with Britain, and he was strapped for money.

The French suddenly began talking about handing over not just part of the Louisiana Territory but all of it. Livingston, who had not been pleased with the arrival of Monroe, feeling it would detract from his credit for any success, consulted his colleague, and the two agreed that they should exceed their instructions and seize the opportunity presenting itself. Livingston met with François de Barbé-Marbois, the French finance minister, whom Napoleon had deputized to negotiate the sale of the Louisiana Territory to the United States. Livingston and Monroe agreed to a total price of $15 million, which included U.S. assumption of claims against the French by American citizens, and the treaty was finalized in May 1803. Livingston subsequently sent word of the matter directly to Madison without conferring with Monroe, which led to the estrangement of the two Republicans.

The United States had struck a tremendous bargain. The Louisiana Purchase, approximately 828,000 square miles, doubled the size of the United States, making it the second largest nation in the world in area and the world leader in tillable soil. The sale also secured the Mississippi River basin for future American development, including natural resources not even imagined. However, the treaty did not specify the final boundaries of the territory, which would not be set for many years.

Monroe, despite his anger with Livingston, had reason to be pleased. As a champion of the West, he had played a part, albeit limited, in the purchase of a region that would be greatly beneficial to both western and American prosperity and security.

DREAD GOD.

More important, a much larger United States possessed a potential for growth that would someday guarantee its emergence as a great power. More than many other leaders, Monroe had a sense of a world power struggle in which the United States had to stand up against the entrenched autocratic monarchies of Europe. Louisiana under Spain had been a power vacuum, attracting the attention of other Europeans. The British, with some ease, could have taken it over at almost any time. Napoleon might have swung back to earlier dreams of a Caribbean-based empire. Jefferson had already suggested that in such cases the United States would have felt obliged to seek alliances to protect its own special interests. But now the nation, much to Monroe's delight, emerged unallied and strengthened.

The Monroe crest. Monroe was of Scottish and Welsh ancestry, but his policies as an American president significantly reduced European influence in the Western Hemisphere.

4

A Treaty Most Repugnant

After Napoleon Bonaparte seized absolute control over the French Revolution in 1799, the authoritarian military regime he instituted had led to a considerable cooling of Republican fervor for the French, and the United States sought better relations with Great Britain. Rufus King, an Adams appointee held over as minister to Britain in the first years of Jefferson's presidency, had proved highly competent in smoothing out points of contention with the British. But in 1803 King was on his way home, and the administration sent Monroe over from Paris to London to take his place.

For Monroe the change must have seemed fitting and somewhat belated. Monroe had been upset when Jefferson's new Republican government had not made a clean sweep of all Federalists in 1801. Yet from the standpoint of the United States, replacing King was not necessarily an improvement. An adroit negotiator, King had been able to build up a network of solid connections in Britain. Monroe, tainted in British eyes by his Francophile sympathies, found his reception in London correct but often cool. From the time of his arrival, diplomatic relations between the two countries turned downward.

> *Monroe arrived in London on July 18, 1803, slightly anxious about the reception awaiting him.*
> —HARRY AMMON
> Monroe biographer

In 1799, officers of the USS *Constellation* force sailors from the French frigate *L'Insurgente* below-decks after one of the confrontations that marked an undeclared naval war between the United States and France.

In 1803, after negotiating the Louisiana Purchase in France, Monroe was sent to London (pictured here) to replace former minister to Britain Rufus King. The British were well aware of Monroe's pro-France sympathies, however, and he was given a cool reception upon arrival in England.

It was not entirely Monroe's fault. During his three-year stay in London, the British government would change four times, necessitating each time a whole new round of efforts to reconcile differences. Jefferson believed that ultimately the pressures of a continuing war with France would lead Britain to seek closer ties with the United States; what Monroe found among the British, however, was not an inclination toward closeness but rather a contempt for American policies and leadership and a difficulty in understanding American objectives, combined with an ongoing arrogance by the British, who saw their government as stronger, more sophisticated, and more just than that of America.

To add to Monroe's difficulties, the Peace of Amiens, the temporary peace between Britain and France that had provided the opportunity for the United States to purchase Louisiana, came to an end, and war between Britain and France resumed in 1803. The Royal Navy took up again its practice of impressing (forcing into service) seamen from neutral ships, including those of the United States, a practice the British considered an internationally accepted and justified ritual of warfare. Americans, on the other hand, considered it a humiliating policy and angrily refused to countenance any surrender of British civilians or seamen who had fled war service in their own country.

British merchants, hard-pressed by years of conflict and disruption, watched angrily as American ships increasingly played the primary role in Atlantic commerce, penetrating the West Indies and Latin America in place not only of British trade but of French as well. American ships steadily built a profitable business plying directly between the French West Indies and France, a business the French had prohibited in peacetime but approved now that the ocean was controlled by the British navy. The British government invoked its Rule of 1756, claiming that trade prohibited to neutral ships in peacetime was equally illegal in war and that any foreign ships engaging in such trade could no longer be considered neutral. The Americans, however, had been using the policy of the "broken passage," in which ships broke a direct route by stopping at a U.S. port, thus circumventing the rule and avoiding seizure.

At the end of 1803, Monroe was ordered to Spain to help the U.S. minister, Charles Pinckney, negotiate for the cession of the Floridas to the United States and the establishment of a western boundary of Louisiana where it bordered Spanish territory. Monroe spent several months there, but, to Jefferson's dismay, the negotiations were unsuccessful. As he had done in France, Monroe revealed some of the traits that set him apart from both Jefferson and Madison. He tended to act as though diplomats were policymakers rather than policy implementers; he seemed to find it hard simply to take orders. In addition, he favored actions that were generally more aggressive than Jefferson and Madison sought. Seeing the weakness of Spain, Monroe urged his government to make demands and threaten dire consequences if American goals were not met. He stubbornly believed that Jefferson and Madison supported his position when in fact they did not, and when thwarted, he tended to view the pursuit of any alternate policy as a personal rebuke.

U.S. minister to Spain, Charles Pinckney. In 1803 Jefferson ordered Monroe to join Pinckney in Spain, where negotiations concerning the Florida territory and the Louisiana border were underway. In Spain, Monroe once again overstepped his diplomatic authority and the negotiations failed.

Conservative British prime minister William Pitt addresses the House of Lords. Under Pitt, the British government maintained a hard-line attitude toward U.S. shipping rights and continued a policy of seizing U.S. vessels and their crews.

Determined to get the Floridas, Jefferson grasped at an alternative plan that would have significant consequences not only for him and the Republican party but for Monroe as well. The French indicated that their government would try to convince their ally Spain to cede the Floridas in return for a cash payment to Spain, and in 1805 Jefferson requested part of the money from Congress. John Randolph of Virginia and a number of other leading Republicans, including John Taylor of Caroline, a senator from Virginia, saw this as a replay of the notorious XYZ Affair of the 1790s, when French officials had sought a bribe from the Adams administration prior to negotiating a resumption of diplomatic relations with the United States. That Jefferson would stoop to such depths appeared immoral to this band of righteous purists, who began to call themselves "Old" Republicans. These critics of Jefferson believed that Monroe's aggressive plan had been the proper one to pursue, and they began to consider Monroe as a candidate for the Republican presidential nomination in 1808.

When Monroe returned to England in July 1805, he found that relations between Britain and the United States were growing increasingly tense. He arrived in the British capital on the same day that the critical *Essex* decision was made, in which the admiralty court held that the Rule of 1756 did indeed apply to ships that made broken passages. The decision required that the owners of any American ship seized by the British for violating the rule produce evidence that they had not intended to skirt it when breaking the movement of goods from the West Indies. American shipping was no longer protected, and the British began to step up seizures of American vessels.

Monroe urged the U.S. government to assert itself vigorously against the ruling. He recommended that restrictive duties be imposed on British imports to the United States and that trade with the British West Indies be cut off entirely. (Jefferson would not adopt this alternative until late in 1807.) Monroe and the administration saw some hope when the conservative British prime minister, William Pitt,

died in January 1806, and the new government appointed as foreign secretary Charles James Fox, who had long been liberal in his approach to Anglo-American relations. Fox attempted to defuse the furor over the *Essex* decision by promising privately, though not publicly, that the government would stop enforcing the rule. On such other vital matters as impressment, however, Fox was in no position to relent.

The war between Britain and France worsened. In 1806, Napoleon established his Continental System, a plan designed to cripple Britain economically and force it out of the war. Using his power and influence over parts of Europe not directly involved in the conflict, the emperor closed one port after another to British goods. Even France, which had indirectly imported considerable quantities of British products, would no longer be a customer. Britain responded with governmental decrees known as the Orders in Council, which declared the European coast under a British blockade and closed to neutral ships. Napoleon announced his own blockade of the

D—n such Liberty and D—n such a flotilla & I tell you we might as well embark in walnut shells.

A British cartoon ridicules Napoleon's Continental System, by which the French emperor coerced weak European nations into aiding France in the war against Britain. Napoleon (left) is pictured bullying Dutchmen into setting sail in a fleet of walnut shells for an invasion of England.

British coast in the Berlin Decree of 1806. His Milan Decree of the following year allowed for the seizure of neutral ships sailing from British ports or colonies. The effect of the reciprocal blockades was to close, theoretically at least, all British and most European ports to American trade and to subject neutral American ships to capture by either Britain or France.

Jefferson and Madison instructed Monroe to make an effort to secure a new treaty with Britain that would put an end to impressment and redefine the British blockade in a way that would be more favorable to the United States. Before Monroe could get started, however, Senator Samuel Smith of Maryland built up support for the idea of sending to London a second envoy, as Jefferson had sent Monroe to France to assist Livingston in 1803. Jefferson dispatched William Pinkney, a distinguished lawyer and outspoken opponent of the Rule of 1756. Now Monroe was in the same position as Livingston had been; he wanted the credit for any successful negotiation and viewed Pinkney as an interloper. Aware of some of the machinations within the Republican party at home, Monroe believed that sending Pinkney was an effort to undercut his chances for the presidency in 1808.

However, Monroe proved more generous than had Livingston. When Pinkney arrived, Monroe welcomed him and set to work with him. Fox, at this point seriously ill, chose two commissioners to represent the British position in the negotiations who were sensitive to the need to placate the United States if possible. Once again Monroe seemed to have a different understanding of American objectives than Madison. The secretary of state believed that an end to impressment was central to the success of any new treaty. Monroe, who had spent a number of years outside the United States but little time in the national capital, never really comprehended the true depth of national humiliation and anger over the issue of impressment. For him the trade aspects of a new treaty were more vital. Monroe could accept assurances from Fox's commissioners, and from a new government formed after Fox's death in September, that while Britain would not publicly end impressment, it would pursue a very restricted practice. Pragmatic though this appeared to him, it hardly fit the sense of justice that Americans desired.

The Monroe-Pinkney draft treaty contained provisions beneficial to the United States: It reinstated the neutrality of goods on a broken passage; gave the United States most-favored-nation status, thus ensuring that no other foreign power would receive trade privileges greater than those granted the United States; and stated that the British would not stop any unarmed ships within five miles of the U.S. coast, thereby effectively protecting American coastal shipping from impressment and saving Americans the embarrassment of British warships within sight of the coast. But other provisions were less appealing. The United States agreed to forgo any commercial restrictions on British trade for 10 years, which meant that the Americans would have no effective means of retaliation should there be British violations of the treaty. The British also attached a proviso at the end stating that the United States had to defy Napoleon's Berlin Decree. Finally, and most damning, the draft said nothing at all explicitly about impressment.

> *[I]t will be considered a hard treaty when it is known. The British commissioners appear to have screwed every article as far as it would bear, to have taken everything and yielded nothing.*
> —THOMAS JEFFERSON
> on the Monroe-Pinkney
> draft treaty

Monroe thought it the best treaty possible under the circumstances and hoped that Jefferson and Madison would agree. He bristled when he learned that without even waiting for the draft he and Pinkney sent to them, Jefferson and Madison, seeing a copy of the document provided by the British minister in Washington, rejected it outright. Jefferson chose to bury the proposal rather than subject it to Senate scrutiny.

In 1807 a new British government under the Duke of Portland came to power and adopted a hard line toward neutral rights. Monroe and Pinkney's attempts to deal with the new foreign secretary, George Canning, broke off when news arrived that the British warship *Leopold*, intent on impressing seamen, had opened fire on an American ship, the *Chesapeake*, when it refused to submit to a search. The attack damaged the ship, inflicting many casualties, and the British impressed four sailors, two of whom were Americans. In December 1807, in response to the *Chesapeake* crisis, Jefferson imposed a total embargo on trade, which ultimately failed because it was too difficult to enforce.

An English cartoonist's interpretation of a confrontation between American and British vessels shows British marines routing a cowardly and disorganized Yankee crew.

BRITISH VALOUR and YANKEE BOASTING or, Shannon versus Chesapeake.

Leaving behind Pinkney (who would stay on in England as the U.S. minister), Monroe returned in December 1807 to a country that largely either ignored or criticized his efforts. His supporters claimed he had been sacrificed by the administration to serve Madison's aspirations for the presidency. Jefferson failed to invite him to the White House for even so much as a friendly resumption of personal relations, and Monroe thought he discerned Madison's hand in his treatment. Only back in Virginia did he find welcome: Randolph, Taylor, and the Old Republicans wanted him to run for the presidency against Madison. Many of his suspicions and mistrusts oppressed him, and he considered writing another defense of his conduct, similar to the apologia he had penned against the Washington administration on his return from France in 1796, but in the end relented. For the moment, he waited.

An officer of the Royal Navy confronts a group of American crewmen who appear ready and able to resist impressment. When Monroe signed a treaty in 1806 that did not guarantee an end to British impressment of American seamen, Jefferson and Madison rejected the agreement outright.

5

Defender of the Republic

In 1808, Monroe stood on the verge of a critical period in his career. Yet the year's developments hardly augured well for his political future. President Jefferson, harassed and embittered after two terms in office and impoverished after a lifetime of public service, announced that he would not seek a third term. The Republican party so dominated national politics by this time that its endorsement for the presidency virtually guaranteed election in the fall.

James Madison commanded the support of most Republicans. He held Jefferson's old post in the State Department and was also ambitious. In an age when it still seemed inelegant, if not improper, for a president to join in the process of picking his successor, Jefferson felt constrained from publicly endorsing Madison. But to the president and most of the powerful leaders of the Republican party,

I have ever viewed Mr. Madison and yourself as two principal pillars of my happiness.
—THOMAS JEFFERSON
to James Monroe

In 1811, Monroe's political ambition was partially realized when President Madison appointed him secretary of state. During the War of 1812 with Great Britain, Monroe became secretary of war, and many credited his leadership with turning the tide of the war in favor of the United States.

In 1807, James Madison was chosen over Monroe as the Republican presidential candidate for the upcoming election. Following this defeat, Monroe did not speak to his old friend Madison for two years.

Madison had the preeminent claim to be Jefferson's heir both because of the greater political prominence he had won as virtual author of the Constitution and because of his experience in the House of Representatives and as a prominent member of the administration. Seven years Monroe's senior, he enjoyed the advantage of seniority, the respect for which was so entrenched in the gentry's code of propriety. On a more personal level, Madison was an older and much closer friend of Jefferson's and, more than Monroe, was the intellectual equal of Jefferson, who shared his interests and ideas.

However, a serious conflict was brewing within the Republican party. A number of discontented men — the Old Republicans or so-called Quids — wanted to see Monroe run for the presidency. Virginians John Randolph and John Taylor of Caroline, among others, had transferred their support to Monroe as far back as 1805, when they believed that Jefferson was both dangerously expanding the powers of the central government and engaging in domestic and foreign policy-making that smacked of immorality. Especially damning to them was Jefferson's 1805 attempt to use funds secretly sought from Congress to "expedite" the securing of the Spanish Floridas at the recommendation of France, which had suggested bribery to Randolph and his allies. Whereas Monroe had long shown himself to be a foe of overly strong national power in the domestic sphere, he was aggressive in foreign affairs. The repudiation by Jefferson and Madison of the Monroe-Pinkney draft treaty in 1806 made Monroe all the more attractive to the malcontents.

In January 1807, a congressional caucus held to name the presidential candidates nominated Madison by an overwhelming margin. The Old Republicans did not attend, nor did the supporters of George Clinton, the governor of New York, who also had presidential ambitions. Monroe's supporters failed to build a strong campaign against Madison. Randolph, a waspish, cantankerous loner and a bitter enemy of Jefferson's, managed to alienate possible support both within and outside of Virginia. And it was only at this point, when Monroe's supporters ran him for president, that Jefferson realized how unhappy Monroe was with the lack of progress in his political career. He wrote to Monroe to assure him that he still valued his protégé's friendship and believed in his ability to serve the country.

Monroe, as befit a candidate at the time, did not campaign on his own behalf, but left the politicking to his champions. In part spurred by his own ambition and his need for vindication from the stigma of failure as a diplomat, in part because he believed that his positions were more authentically Republican than Madison's, and in part because he felt an obligation to those who supported him, Monroe did not withdraw. He was not even swayed by a guarded appeal from Jefferson to defer. For reasons that are not clear, Monroe now stopped all communication with Madison, and they would not be in contact again for more than two years. Monroe's obstinacy seemingly should have forever sundered his longtime association with Jefferson and Madison. Some Republicans never forgave him his mute defiance of his seniors, but both men forgave him over time. Jefferson maintained his friendship even through the election. Monroe's relationship with Madison took longer to heal, but eventually the two corresponded again.

"Old Republican" John Randolph of Virginia. The Old Republicans were an anti-Jefferson faction within the Republican party, formed in 1905 in response to corruption and federalist tendencies within the Jefferson administration.

Senator John Taylor of Carolina was one of the Old Republicans, who supported Monroe as the Republican presidential candidate for the 1808 election. The Old Republicans ran a lackluster campaign, however, and Monroe was defeated by James Madison.

Madison soundly defeated Monroe in Virginia, thus ensuring his election. Monroe's poor showing at the polls brought his political life to a temporary halt. Away from politics, he could devote more time to his family and his plantation, Highland, in Ablemarle County, Virginia. He had bought the 3,500-acre property, located next to Jefferson's estate, Monticello, right before he had left for France. Now he borrowed money to make improvements on the simple one-story house he had built earlier. His main crop was tobacco, but he imported vines from Bordeaux, France, to satisfy a growing interest in the cultivation of grapes.

In September 1808, Monroe's eldest daughter, Eliza, married George Hay, a well-known Virginia lawyer, who would become his father-in-law's lifelong supporter and adviser. Madison was conspicuous by his absence. Whenever the new president visited nearby Monticello, Monroe always stayed away, and the Madisons never paid a social call to Highland. Jefferson did his best to reconcile the two men; he even delivered news of possible political appointments Madison was considering for Monroe. But Monroe thought the posts offered beneath him, feeling that, given his experience, he deserved nothing less than a cabinet position. He had only to wait, for by the spring of 1810, he had good reason to expect such a post.

From the beginning of his presidency, Madison had encountered opposition from a powerful congressional faction led by Senator William Branch Giles of Virginia and Maryland senator Samuel Smith. In 1809 the president was defeated in his attempt to appoint as secretary of state Albert Gallatin, former secretary of the Treasury. Madison considered Monroe for the post, but he proved equally unacceptable to the senators. Madison did not yet have enough support to alienate these powerful men, and to placate them, he named Robert Smith, Senator Smith's brother, as secretary of state. The president reconciled himself to a Smith in the State Department, but he never forgave the senator and his allies for thwarting him.

Monroe sensed that the time was right for him to return to politics. In April 1810, he easily won election to the Virginia House of Delegates. The following month, Monroe and Madison were reconciled when Monroe went to Washington to clarify his diplomatic accounts. Monroe remained popular enough in Virginia to serve again as governor in the early months of 1811, when Governor John Tyler resigned to accept a judgeship. By that spring, Madison felt politically strong enough to rid his government of the Smith family influence when Senator Smith and his clique opposed his wish to send Joel Barlow, a party stalwart and well-known Francophile, as an emissary to France. The president not only got Barlow approved but forced the resignation of Secretary of State Smith in the bargain. This time Madison picked someone he wanted: James Monroe.

Monticello (pictured here), Jefferson's estate in Ablemarle, Virginia, bordered Highland, Monroe's plantation. Following his unsuccessful bid for the presidency in 1807, Monroe spent a period of temporary retirement at Highland.

Monroe inherited a tense situation. In 1810, Congress had passed Macon's Bill No. 2, which authorized trade with both Britain and France until one of the two belligerents withdrew its trade restrictions against neutral shipping. Then the United States would reinstitute a policy of nonintercourse — the cessation of all trade — with the uncooperative nation. That fall, Napoleon, in a slyly worded declaration that was officially delivered through his foreign minister, appeared to revoke the French restrictions on U.S. shipping that had been outlined in his Berlin and Milan decrees. Madison invoked Macon's Bill No. 2 against Britain. Britain protested, contending that Napoleon had neither revoked his decrees nor had ordered the French to stop preying on American shipping. Britain would not repeal its restriction policy, the Orders in Council, until there was proof the French had really ended their policy.

Madison and Monroe were willing to accept a concrete act on Britain's part, the cessation of its implementation of the Orders in Council, without the necessity of a public declaration that it had ended its practices. Moreover, they did not demand an immediate end to impressment. In early 1811, the new British foreign minister to Washington, Sir Augustus John Foster, arrived. He considered the United States a third-rate power, did not conceal his feelings, and soon alienated Monroe. In July, Foster delivered a formal protest against the nonintercourse policy aimed at Britain. He brought up other British complaints, including U.S. activity in East Florida (held by Britain's ally Spain) and the *Little Belt* incident, in which a U.S. warship fired on a British naval vessel, but Monroe stated that no minor issues would be addressed until Britain revoked the Orders in Council.

In October, Monroe returned to Washington from a vacation to find the situation worse. Barlow reported an increasing strain in U.S.-French relations, and negotiations with the British were stalled. By May 1812, war with Britain seemed inevitable. Madison felt strongly the pressure from many Americans, mostly Republicans in the South

Henry Clay of Kentucky. By 1812 tensions between the United States and Great Britain had again reached the flash point. President Madison attempted to maintain a conciliatory policy, but war hawks such as Clay felt that American honor was at stake and urged Madison to declare war.

and West, who resented Britain's highhandedness in dealing with American shipping and its slap at U.S. national honor and pride. The "War Hawks" in Congress — powerful newcomers such as Henry Clay of Kentucky and John C. Calhoun of South Carolina — favored confrontation over submission. In June 1812, by a largely partisan and sectional vote in Congress, the United States declared war on Great Britain.

With the outbreak of war, Monroe saw less to be gained from his State Department post than from involvement in the military operations. When William Eustis of Massachusetts, a precinct politician ill prepared for the job, withdrew as secretary of war, Madison moved Monroe to that post. When the Senate balked at accepting Monroe's transfer to the War Department — it felt that too many Virginians occupied the important government posts — Madison appointed Monroe acting secretary of war. In the 10 weeks he served in that position, Monroe pushed for expansion of the army and proposed a plan for the invasion of Canada, still a British colony. However, Madison returned him to the State Department when he appointed John Armstrong of New York as secretary of war.

First Lady Dolley Madison, with the Declaration of Independence safely in hand, flees the presidential mansion on the night of the British invasion of the capital, August 24, 1814. The British troops set much of the city on fire, and the presidential mansion, among other government buildings, was burned to the ground.

Armstrong, who had presidential ambitions, blocked Monroe's hopes for military glory. He prevented Monroe's appointment to command the army for the invasion of Canada and assumed the role himself. Monroe, who normally was able to work with his opponents even if he did not like them, found himself unable to tolerate Armstrong.

Fortunately, Monroe soon had State Department affairs to occupy his attention. In early 1813, he received an offer from Tsar Alexander I of Russia to mediate the dispute between the United States and Great Britain, which Madison quickly accepted. A three-man commission, made up of John Quincy Adams (then U.S. minister to Russia), Albert Gallatin, and a Delaware Federalist, James A. Bayard, was sent to Russia for talks. In December 1813, Madison received a message from British foreign minister Lord Castlereagh suggesting direct negotiations, and Monroe encouraged him to accept. Monroe and Madison made clear that the end of impressment was essential to any peace settlement.

Monroe's most dramatic moment of the war came in 1814. On August 16, British ships appeared at the mouth of the Potomac River. Ignoring Armstrong (who would only last another month as war secretary), Madison took personal charge of operations in the region. He created a new military district that included parts of Virginia and Maryland, together with the District of Columbia, and placed it under the command of Brigadier General William H. Winder. Together with Winder and Monroe, Madison directed the military operations.

Less than a week later, after they drove a small American naval force from the Chesapeake, the British routed the Americans on land at Bladensburg, Maryland. So quickly did the Americans run away that the battle got the ignominious title of the "Bladensburg Races." Madison and Monroe had visited General Winder's positions outside Washington as the British approached, and Monroe oversaw the repositioning of some of the forces.

British warships bombard Fort McHenry in an attempt to capture Baltimore on September 13, 1814. Under the direction of the new secretary of war — Monroe — the city was staunchly defended by American troops and the British were forced to abandon their assault.

On August 24, 1814, the British seized Washington. Most of the government had fled; Madison and Monroe went to Virginia, and Winder returned to Maryland to regroup. In Washington the British set fire to the president's mansion and proceeded to methodically put to the torch all government buildings, including the Capitol. The only building spared was the Patent Office. The United States had reached a nadir in its quest for affirmation of its rights and honor.

After 24 hours the British withdrew from the capital, heading north into Maryland. The government returned, and Congress immediately engaged in a series of lengthy debates over whether Washington should be abandoned for the time being until its security could be assured. Monroe must have been reminded of the dark days of the Revolution, when another Congress had fled the capital at Philadel-

phia and then debated its future. Fortunately both houses finally voted to remain. Madison sent Armstrong on a "vacation" to New York: In a week, the secretary of war resigned. Monroe was again named acting secretary of war. He had a cot brought to his office, where he stayed to formulate plans for the defense of the next likely target, Baltimore. The subsequent vigorous and successful defense of Baltimore (with the famous attack that inspired Francis Scott Key's poem "The Star-Spangled Banner"), together with news of U.S. victories on the Great Lakes, brought new hope to the disheartened capital. Monroe's leadership in the War Department helped enhance his reputation, increasing his stature as presidential material for 1816.

In the waning months of the war, one of his concerns was for the Gulf Coast. From information he had received in early September, he believed that

The bloody Battle of New Orleans, in which 5,300 British infantrymen marched directly into the withering fire of General Andrew Jackson's entrenched troops, many of whom were expert Kentucky and Tennessee sharpshooters. Within 30 minutes the British suffered 2,036 casualties; Jackson's troops suffered only 31.

A cartoon view of the 1814 Hartford convention, at which several New England states gathered to propose amendments to the Constitution that would limit federal authority in matters of international conflict. However, news of Jackson's victory at New Orleans overshadowed the demands of the New Englanders.

the British were planning a strike against the crucial port city of New Orleans. He ordered General Andrew Jackson, commanding in the South, to rush to New Orleans. Monroe sent troops and promised additional weapons. Jackson delayed, and Monroe's promised supplies got held up, but in the end Jackson reached New Orleans in time to win a stunning victory against the British on January 8, 1815, one that won him a glorious reputation.

As it turned out, however, the Battle of New Orleans was technically unnecessary. Both sides wanted to end the war: Britain was exhausted from the long conflict with Napoleon, and the United States, its capital city now in ruins, did not want to deplete its resources any further. Two weeks before Jackson's victory the American negotiators at Ghent, Belgium — John Quincy Adams, Albert Gallatin, and Henry Clay — had met with a team of British diplomats and worked out a peace agreement. The Treaty of Ghent essentially restored the situation in North America to its pre-1812 condition. Though neither side made any territorial gains and the issues of freedom of the seas and impressment were left moot, Monroe felt that America had been victorious nonetheless. The nation had refused to be bullied and had fought for its rights and reputation. Most important for Monroe was that the republic had survived.

Before he surrendered his War Department post to resume again his duties as secretary of state, Monroe tried unsuccessfully to get Congress to commit the United States to maintaining a substantial peacetime army. He returned to the State Department in March 1815 and began the process of settling issues left unsettled at Ghent that would lead, in 1817, to the Rush-Bagot Agreement with Britain, another effort to resolve outstanding points of controversy between the two countries over Britain's presence in Canada. Monroe's thoughts also turned more and more to the following year and the national elections that would determine a successor to Madison. The secretary of state had reason to be pleased. His blessed republic had endured. Not only had the British been kept at bay, but a brief and sour episode involving the New England states, in which some Federalists had talked of secession, had ended to his satisfation. In 1814, a convention of New England states at Hartford, Connecticut, had drawn up a list of proposed amendments to the Constitution to protect the states from the war-making powers of the national government. Alas for the Hartfordians, news of Jackson's glorious victory reached Washington just as their delegation did, and they were ignored. Monroe, the consummate nationalist in matters of national honor and prestige, could only look ahead with pleasure and confidence.

> *The demonstration is satisfactory that our Union has gained strength, our troops honor, and the nation character, by the contest.*
> —JAMES MONROE
> on the War of 1812

6

President of Good Feelings

James Monroe had every reason to believe that he would be the Republican choice for president in 1816 and that his election was a foregone conclusion. In part owing to its opposition to the war, the Federalist party had lost its ability to command a significant national following. The Hartford Convention debacle signaled the end of the party as a national force, leaving it largely a sectional remnant in New England. Moreover, Monroe was Madison's and Jefferson's choice for chief executive, though, following tradition, Madison did not openly announce a preference.

Monroe found himself facing two opposition groups. The powerful New York Republicans resented the long monopoly by Virginians of the presidency and key cabinet posts. They believed that Jefferson and Madison had used the State Department to launch their successors, and they hoped to end the "Virginia Dynasty" in 1816. The New York Republicans favored the state's wartime governor, Daniel Tompkins, who was not nationally known.

> *The nation has become tired of the follies of faction.*
> —NICHOLAS BIDDLE
> a friend of Monroe's, after his election

Following the War of 1812, Monroe found himself in an excellent position to make a run for the presidency. His conduct as secretary of war during the British invasion had won him wide public acclaim, and both Madison and Jefferson were ready to back him as the Republican candidate.

Daniel Tompkins, who had been the governor of New York during the War of 1812, represented one of the obstacles to Monroe's presidential intentions. Tompkins had the backing of the powerful New York Republicans, who wanted to elect a president from their own state rather than another Virginian.

A more serious threat to Monroe came from the supporters of Georgian William Crawford, Madison's secretary of the Treasury, who was extremely popular with important congressmen from the South and West as well as with conservative Republicans. Crawford's supporters especially opposed the establishment of a federal bank, which Monroe favored, and they saw Monroe as the champion of Old Republicanism, which he had abandoned as long ago as 1811.

Monroe's managers were sufficiently worried that he might not carry the party caucus that they toyed with the idea of boycotting the caucus and appealing directly to state legislatures for his nomination. Monroe was more familiar to state leaders than either Crawford or Tompkins. But his backers finally decided to risk the normal caucus procedure.

Neither Monroe's nor Crawford's managers felt sure of victory, and at the first caucus call in early March 1816, less than half of the Republicans in Congress turned up, not enough to hold a vote. A second call, for March 16, produced a better showing: 119 Republicans attended. By common agreement (to placate the New Yorkers), Tompkins was nominated as the party's vice-presidential candidate. Crawford knew that Madison favored Monroe, and as the younger of the two candidates, he believed he could wait. He did not publicly stand against Monroe (believing, he claimed in 1824, that he had a tacit promise from Monroe to support him as his successor), but he also did not publicly withdraw from contention. It was a close race: When the caucus votes were counted, Monroe received 65 to Crawford's 54. This embarrassment to Monroe may help explain his profound silence, private as well as public, when Crawford sought his support as his successor in 1824.

The election campaign of 1816 was virtually an anticlimax. The Federalists ran Rufus King of New York against Monroe in a campaign that seemed nothing more than a formality. Not only did neither candidate campaign, which was not unusual, but no one else did much campaigning in their behalf, and no contentious political rhetoric filled the air. Monroe carried almost the entire nation, receiving 183 electoral votes to King's 34. (King carried only Massachusetts, Connecticut, and Delaware.)

Rufus King, Monroe's Federalist opponent in the 1816 election. The Federalists had fallen out of favor with the public, and Monroe was elected president in a landslide victory.

Madison's last months in office saw the creation of legislation that would have been anathema to Republicans in the 1790s (and still was to some). Madison approved the creation of a new federal bank, the Second Bank of the United States, to replace Alexander Hamilton's creation, the First Bank, whose charter had not been renewed in 1811. He also agreed to a protective tariff, the first in American history. Madison had never opposed business per se but only business development that might overshadow the basic agrarian economy of the United States and replace it with mere luxury and speculation. By 1816, Monroe believed that the increasingly strong nation he envisioned required the sort of economic growth encouraged by the new legislation, and he supported it. He felt that the achievements of Madison's last months in office largely addressed the issue of governmental encouragement of business enterprise and now the country only required a cautious caretaker to assure the political stability upon which economic growth depended.

This fit neatly into his conception of the presidency, one that previous presidents had shared, but perhaps none with greater determination than the man who took the oath early in March 1817. Monroe felt that presidents should concern themselves with the conduct of foreign affairs and the formation of foreign policy (for which the diplomatic service and secretaryship of state had prepared him). Chief executives should also competently administer the domestic policies set forth by the Congress, which reflected the public's will, and not attempt to interpose their own preferences. Finally, the nation required a president who, through personal dignity and restraint, elevated the office and the country. Few disputed Monroe's projection of that dignity. Dressed in the 18th-century style, with knee breeches and buckled shoes and wearing a long, somber cloth coat, with his hair powdered and drawn at the back into a queue, Monroe reminded the public of the greatness of America's origins in the Revolution. At times he even put on his old army uniform.

For his cabinet, Monroe chose highly competent administrators for key posts. He wanted to divide the positions among men from different geographic regions in order to achieve a truly national representation. Monroe appointed John Quincy Adams of Massachusetts, the seasoned diplomat and former Federalist who had converted to the Republican cause, as secretary of state. Monroe might have picked a lesser talent, someone unlikely to threaten his own diplomatic reputation, but instead he chose the man he thought most qualified for the job. It was, however, as close as Monroe came to naming any Federalist to an important office. Although he declared that he believed the country could do without political parties, he had no desire to reward enemies or deprive friends.

James Monroe is sworn in as the president of the United States in an inaugural ceremony held in Washington, D.C., in March 1817. Perhaps more than any previous chief executive, the tall and dignified Monroe presented a truly presidential image to the public.

William Crawford of Georgia, the influential secretary of the Treasury in the Madison administration, was appointed to the same position in Monroe's cabinet in spite of the fact that Monroe held a grudge against him.

Monroe's hopes for a cross-section of the nation in his cabinet were dashed when Henry Clay, his "western" choice, rejected the president's offer of the secretaryship of the War Department. (Clay had had his eyes on the State Department.) John C. Calhoun of South Carolina, who, along with Clay, had been one of the War Hawks seeking war with Britain in 1812, accepted the post Clay turned down. For the Treasury Department, Monroe held over William Crawford, a man too powerful to be challenged. The only other Madison administration holdover, Benjamin Crowninshield of Massachusetts, who headed the Navy Department, quit his office in 1818, the only member of the cabinet to leave during Monroe's two terms. It was a government of greatly talented — and very ambitious — men. Writing in his diary of Monroe's administration, John Quincy Adams would convey the picture of a president with considerable skill in harnessing and directing the diverse and contending personalities.

Unity, harmony, and stability were Monroe's objectives not only for the government but throughout the nation. In his first inaugural address, given on March 4, 1817, Monroe called the American people "one great family with a common interest." He stressed the need for a strong national defense and the encouragement of industry and commerce, including building up manufacturing to make the United States independent of foreign imports. Although not an impressive public speaker, Monroe won praise for his plain style and straightforwardness.

In an attempt to foster a rapprochement between the Federalists and the national government, Monroe decided to emulate President Washington and personally tour the country. He wanted to give the Federalists, whose reputation was badly tarnished, a chance to join in supporting the new government.

Political and economic prosperity flourished during the first months of Monroe's presidency. The new president toured the nation and succeeded in uniting Federalists and Republicans in a spirit of national harmony and good will.

He announced that his objective was to examine military fortifications and frontier outposts, and to allay possible criticism of a politically motivated charade, he determined to pay his expenses out of his own pocket, forgoing such frills as a military escort. In June 1817 he began his tour by heading northward.

The welcome he received must have been extremely gratifying to a man who yearned for recognition of his many services to the public. Federalist as well as Republican local and state officials overwhelmed him with hospitality (save for the Federalist governor of New Hampshire, William Plumer, who refused to call out the militia to accompany the president through the state). Monroe traveled to Baltimore, Philadelphia, and New York, with a side trip to Trenton, the site of his revolutionary war heroism. The most memorable moment of the trip north came when Monroe reached Boston, the stronghold of Federalism, to help celebrate the Fourth of July. A crowd of 40,000 turned out to cheer him, and Federalist officials went to great lengths to welcome him. A Boston Federalist paper, the *Columbian Centinel*, would classify the time as an "era of good feelings." The phrase caught on, was repeated, and ultimately became synonymous with Monroe's presidency. Considering the conflicts and crises of the months and years that followed, the epithet turned out to be misleading.

Monroe and his family settled into White House life. In 1819 the president decided to erect a larger house at Oak Hill, Virginia, which was closer to the capital than Highland, so that he could spend his summers in Virginia while his cabinet secretaries stayed in Washington. The new White House family was a very different one from the Madisons, much more formal and dignified, as befit Monroe's notions of his and his family's position. Former first lady Dolley Madison had been known for her warmth and lively social sense. Elizabeth Monroe, on the other hand, was seen as cool and reserved. Unlike her predecessor, she did not venture out to make calls on the wives of congressmen and diplomats; she only received visitors.

For his part, Monroe, who had spent years at the formal, protocol-bound courts of Europe, declared that all diplomats would henceforth be received by him only on official occasions. He felt that the president should not appear to form friendships with some diplomats over others and that it was beneath the dignity of his office to allow foreign officials to simply drop in at the White House on a social call. Although he tended to preserve a stiff correctness at formal gatherings, Monroe broke through his public reserve at more informal events, such as small dinner parties, where his personal warmth, friendliness, and sense of humor sometimes surprised his guests.

The unity, harmony, and stability Monroe sought for his administration proved ephemeral at best. By 1819 the wave of postwar prosperity that had swept Europe and the United States after Napoleon's final defeat in 1815 began to recede. The growth had been fueled by purchases of items not available while the war had raged, by uncontrolled land speculation, and by investment and buying inspired by

Napoleon (on white horse) gives a final address to his loyal Old Guard before the Battle of Waterloo. The emperor's defeat in the subsequent battle marked the end of his domination of Europe and the beginning of the brief period of prosperity that accompanied Monroe's first months in office.

the prospect of unlimited sales. Even the new Bank of the United States could not resist the temptation and overextended itself by plunging into the speculative boom in futures on farms, town sites, and merchant enterprises, rooted in the promise of ever-expanding markets for goods and services. But the purchases fell off in time, the markets contracted, and prices, instead of riding higher on a surge of confidence, fell off. Borrowers suddenly could not service (meet interest payments on) or repay debts, and banks that had overextended credit to customers were unable to balance their books. Many of them had to close their doors or foreclose on mortgages and loans in hopes of turning land and buildings into quick cash.

The train of failures and closures and dashed hopes came crashing down in the Panic of 1819, which in turn signaled the start of a prolonged recession that would last three years. Particularly hard hit were the West and South, where many came to blame and resent the national bank. The federal government saw a drop in revenue, much of which came from customs duties. Hampered by the commonly accepted limited role of the national government in economic affairs, Monroe could not do much about the recession. In his 1820 annual message, he urged people to view the situation as temporary, as the result of a natural decline in growth after the frenzied postwar years, and to be frugal and industrious. He basically suggested that they wait out the bad times.

On top of the crash and recession came a crisis that gave the nation the first bitter taste of the division between North and South that would ultimately split the country. In February 1819, legislation came to Congress to enable Missouri, part of the Louisiana Purchase, to become a state. Missouri wanted to be admitted to the Union as a slave state. At the time, the country was equally divided between slave and free states; the acceptance of Missouri would upset the balance, but it was the constitutional right of the people of Missouri to decide what kind of state they wanted to have.

[The Union was saved] by the patriotic devotion of several members in the nonslave-owning states, who preferred the sacrifice of themselves at home to a violation of the obvious principles of the Constitution.

—JAMES MONROE
on the Missouri
Compromise

First Lady Elizabeth Kortright Monroe accompanied her husband on his triumphant tour of the United States following his election. The public responded favorably to the first lady, who seemed naturally suited to her new position.

Representative James Tallmadge of New York attached an amendment to the enabling legislation (that is, the bill introduced to make Missouri a state) to forbid the introduction of more slaves into Missouri and to free children born to slaves in that state when they reached the age of 25. A furor ensued in which passionate pro- and antislavery arguments rocked Congress and the country. Historian Merrill D. Peterson writes, "The amendment started a political storm. It raised serious questions about the constitutional authority of Congress, the nature of the Union, the future of the West, the morality of slavery, and the sectional balance of power."

The Missouri question was only resolved through the patient efforts of congressional leaders, especially Henry Clay, that resulted in the Missouri Compromise. The central part of the compromise provided for the admission of Missouri as a slave state together with the entrance of Maine as a free one, thus maintaining the balance. Slavery was henceforth prohibited in the rest of the Louisiana Purchase north of Missouri's southern boundary, thus making Missouri the only slave state north of that line.

President Monroe did not intervene in the debates and compromises, considering such matters appropriate to the legislative, not the executive, branch. As the product of a slave state, Monroe might have been accused of favoring the widest possible spread of slavery in the interest of slave owners and the southern way of life. Yet it needs to be remembered that he thoroughly disliked the institution of slavery *in the long term* and wished for its *eventual* extinction. Along with Jefferson and Madison, he held the peculiar theory of "diffusion," the watering down of the slave population by spreading slaves over a larger land area. Only then according to the theory would fears among whites be so diminished and the prospect of dealing with a small percentage of freed blacks so unchallenging that manumission would become the vogue and the institution would come to a natural end.

Monroe signed the final statehood bill on the sort of pragmatic grounds that sometimes appealed to

A Dutch man-of-war departs after unloading a shipment of African slaves at Jamestown, Virginia. The issue of slavery would become increasingly prominent during Monroe's term as president.

him. He believed that the challenge to Missouri's admission represented not a genuine moral controversy within the country but only a political confrontation between southern and northern political forces. Monroe believed that should either section seem to win a total victory, the end result would be nationally divisive. By giving the South a partial victory (slavery in Missouri) and the North a partial victory (exclusion of slavery from the rest of the northern part of the Louisiana Purchase), the bill adroitly defused the confrontation and saved national unity and harmony.

In December 1820, Monroe ran for the presidency unopposed and was elected to a second term. The panic and Missouri statehood would end up being the two major domestic crises of his eight years in office. Despite the bitterness of the Missouri issue and the hardships caused by the recession, it seemed that Monroe was determined to whistle bravely no matter what the crisis. In his second inaugural address, in March 1821, the president declared that the country had experienced "no serious conflict" (though Jefferson had privately been profoundly frightened by the Missouri controversy, and John Adams had talked of possible northern secession), and he hoped the recession would prove to be short-lived and insignificant. The British minister to the United States, listening to Monroe's address, noted that several times some unfavorable sounds were heard from the visitors' gallery.

In his quiet, cautious way Monroe did have some input into domestic policy-making. He let it be known that he favored moderate tinkering with existing practices and programs, modest changes in tax schedules, and restrained investment in public projects. He even wrote an important defense of justified internal improvements. In the end he played the role he intended to play as president — dignified, aloof, inconspicuous in domestic affairs, less likely to leave his mark on internal matters than on foreign policy and practice. If the "good feelings" did not last — and they did not — Monroe felt that he could hardly bear the blame, given his moderation in all things.

James Monroe after his election to a second term in office in 1820. The most important national — and moral — issue to come before Monroe during his first term was slavery; Monroe used the Missouri Compromise to sidestep the issue.

7

Mr. Monroe's Doctrine

Unquestionably, the strong side of the Monroe presidency lay in the administration's efforts and achievements in foreign policy. In some measure this must be attributed to the intelligence and determination of the secretary of state, John Quincy Adams, a man possessed by a continental, even a hemispheric, vision of American territoriality and power. Yet Monroe selected Adams and supported him, at critical points even led him, and Adams not only remained loyal and supportive of the president but credited Monroe with qualities of leadership and innovation important to the final results. Adams realized that Monroe shared his desire to raise the United States to a position of prominence in the world.

An early opportunity to pursue the acquisition of Spanish Florida presented itself in 1817, when the Monroe administration contended that the ruling Spanish were not living up to their commitment,

The most important over-all object of [Monroe's] foreign policy was to ensure the recognition of the United States . . . as the strongest power in the Americas.
—HARRY AMMON
Monroe biographer

Uncle Sam straddles the Americas in this cartoon depicting the Monroe Doctrine, which in 1823 became an important part of American foreign policy. The doctrine asserted that any military intrusion into the Western Hemisphere would be considered a threat to the United States.

General Andrew Jackson was only too glad to pursue marauding Seminole Indians across the border into Spanish Florida. After encroaching on the Spanish territory, Jackson decided to claim it for the United States.

outlined in Pinckney's Treaty of 1795, to control the Seminole Indian population of Florida and prevent Indian forays into the American South. Monroe had orders sent to General Andrew Jackson to proceed against the Indians and to pursue them into Spanish territory, if necessary, to restore order. But Jackson was not to attack Indians who had found refuge in Spanish forts.

Jackson, however, had already sent a letter to Monroe stating that, if given the orders, he would occupy East Florida, using the Indian raids as an excuse. He urged Monroe to let him seize Florida and thus present the Spanish with a *fait accompli*, which could then be traded for vital concessions from Spain. Jackson asked that authority be transmitted to him unofficially.

Monroe claimed later, and even signed a deposition to the effect shortly before his death, that he had been ill when Jackson's letter was presented to him by Secretary of War Calhoun and that he had not read it then or for over a year afterward. If true, then Calhoun presumably read Jackson's letter and failed to act immediately on it, possibly assuming that Jackson would obey the orders recently sent him. Jackson later contended that he had received a letter from Representative John Rhea of Tennessee informing him that President Monroe agreed with his aggressive plan. Jackson also claimed that Monroe had later asked him to dispose of the Rhea letter.

In June 1818, Monroe began to see disturbing reports in the press about Jackson's Florida campaign. Monroe waited for official word from Florida, which confirmed the alarming news. In April, Jackson had ordered the execution of two British subjects for purportedly inciting the Indians. A month later he had seized Pensacola, driving out the Spanish governor and his men, who fled to Havana, Cuba.

Initially pleased with Jackson's early success in Florida against the Seminoles, members of Monroe's cabinet flew into an uproar when news arrived about Pensacola and the executions. Not only had Jackson committed an overtly hostile act against Spain, he had drawn Great Britain into the affair. Calhoun at this point claimed that Jackson had knowingly disobeyed the orders sent him to stay away from Spanish posts. Most of the cabinet joined him in wanting to censure the general. Only Secretary Adams saw an advantage in Jackson's achievements, maintaining that control of Florida,

Ships carry the Seminoles away from their Florida homeland. The Seminoles were confined to reservations after Spain ceded Florida to the United States in 1819. They rose up against the U.S. government again in 1835, and after a six-year war the tribe was coerced into relocating to Oklahoma.

The lush Florida swamps became part of the United States on February 24, 1819. In ceding Florida, Spain relinquished one of its last colonial footholds in North America.

which many believed must inevitably belong to the United States, gave the administration a powerful position from which to bargain. Monroe carefully worded a note to the Spanish minister, Don Diego Onís, who was demanding an explanation. Monroe acknowledged that Jackson had gone beyond his authority, but, he claimed, the actions of the Spanish officials on the scene had justified what the general had done. By treading this neutral ground, Monroe masterfully put himself in the best position possible. The United States held Florida, and Monroe avoided publicly censuring a national hero. He ordered the seized forts returned to Spain and told Adams to begin talks on the cession of East Florida to the United States.

On February 24, 1819, Monroe signed the treaty between the United States and Spain that would transfer Florida to the United States. Spain renounced all claims to West Florida (already seized by American settlers in 1810) and ceded East Florida. But the treaty went further, largely owing to Adams, who wanted a kind of omnibus solution that also addressed Spain's presence in the western part of North America. The new treaty for the first time clearly defined the western boundary of the Louisiana Purchase, something Monroe and Livingston had not been able to do with the French back in 1803. Adams wanted a more generous slice of the Southwest, one that would include most of Texas, but Monroe had less interest in that region than in Florida and finally convinced Adams to take what Spain was offering rather than drag on the negotiations. Spain surrendered any claims it had to territory north of California, thus removing one colonial presence from the Pacific Northwest.

When Spain finally ratified the Adams-Onís Treaty in 1821, President Monroe saw that a barrier to another of his aspirations had been removed. Until that time he felt he could not jeopardize the treaty by asking Congress to extend recognition to the new republics emerging south of the United States in what is now Central and South America. They were a result of the fact that Spain, long in decline, had largely lost the ability to maintain its empire, and a number of Latin American leaders had seized upon its weakness to launch independence movements. To the advantage of the United States, Great Britain's objectives regarding Latin America largely corresponded to those of the United States. Though British leaders saw the United States as a competitor for hegemony in the Western Hemisphere and for trade that was bound to grow with newly liberated Latin American states, they in no way wished to strengthen other European countries (especially France) that might choose to intervene in Spain's behalf to prevent the success of independence in the Spanish New World. It suited Britain that France and the other European states be checked in their ambitions and that Latin America develop as a domain accessible to British traders. The British position was crucial, because Britain controlled the Atlantic by virtue of its superior navy.

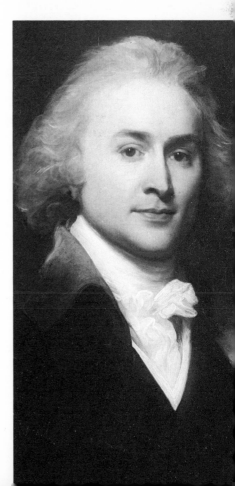

Monroe's brilliant secretary of state, John Quincy Adams, the son of former U.S. president John Adams. John Quincy Adams was the man who was most responsible for the successful implementation of the Monroe Doctrine policies.

This cartoon characterizes the Monroe Doctrine from the European point of view: European potentates watch helplessly as U.S. naval strength grows. One of the doctrine's provisions stated that the United States would not interfere in a European war.

Monroe had a more sympathetic attitude toward these fledgling new states than did Adams, who mistrusted their claims of republicanism, believing that their military origins and Roman Catholic cultures made it difficult for them to adopt republican institutions and practice republican virtues. Monroe chose to accept the new countries as emulators of the United States's republican example, and in 1822 he recommended the formal recognition of the newly independent Latin American nations. By the end of the year, Congress recognized Colombia and Mexico. Recognition of Chile, Argentina, Brazil, and Peru would follow.

Monroe's pragmatic side surfaced to temper his idealism. He did not want to go too far and incite greater Spanish efforts to recover Latin America, nor did he wish to expose the United States to possible war with Spain or other European countries. Moreover, a cardinal tenet of American policy since George Washington's days had been "no entangling alliances." Monroe considered recognition adequate and did not attempt to obtain from Congress financial or military assistance for the new states.

But the matter did not rest there. In October 1823, Secretary Adams showed Monroe dispatches received from Richard Rush, the American minister in London. The French had just put Ferdinand VII back on the Spanish throne after a short-lived revolution in Spain. The restored monarchy might encourage Spain, with France's help, to attempt to regain her lost colonies in the New World. The British foreign minister, George Canning, unofficially invited the Americans to join in issuing a joint statement opposing this possibility.

Monroe was torn. Canning seemed to be offering the United States the chance to share in a major international agreement, one that could elevate the United States in the eyes of the world as a kind of partner to the powerful British. Yet he had some misgivings, especially that the United States might be seen as a subordinate, junior partner while Britain took the lion's share of the credit for launching the initiative, thus enhancing its reputation among the Latin American revolutionaries. Monroe wrote to Jefferson and Madison to gather their impressions. Both encouraged him to accept Canning's proposal. But rather than follow their advice or even share their viewpoints with his cabinet, Monroe merely took their replies under advisement.

The president began official consideration of the offer with his cabinet on November 7. Calhoun, who genuinely feared imminent European intervention, favored the joint Anglo-American approach. Adams was convinced that the Europeans would not interfere, and he must have strengthened Monroe's inclination to reject Canning's offer when he said the United States would appear to be a mere cockboat in the wake of a British man-of-war. Adams wanted to see the United States set forth an independent position, the framework of which he had presented the previous July in response to the presence of Russian settlers in the Pacific Northwest. Adams had declared that not only did the Russians have no right to any land on the continent but that "the American continents . . . [were] henceforth not to be considered as subject for future colonization by any European power."

It was at this modest desk that the principles determining both the political and economic balance of the Western Hemisphere in the 19th and 20th centuries were formulated. The desk is on exhibit in Fredericksburg, Virginia.

By mid-November the Anglo-American resolution became a dead issue when Rush notified Adams that Canning was no longer interested in a joint declaration. But Monroe felt that some sort of public declaration of policy regarding Latin America was desirable. At a cabinet meeting on November 21, another element was added to the policy declarations being considered. Seeing the conflict between republicanism and autocracy as worldwide, Monroe launched an attack on France's intervention in Spanish politics and proposed as well that the United States recognize and send a minister to Greece, which was fighting for independence from the Turks. The Greeks, considered the originators of democracy, were a popular cause among Americans. However, Adams cautioned Monroe that such statements would be provocative to Europeans and not consistent with the United States's feeling that Europeans should stay out of the politics of the Americas.

On November 25, Monroe read to his cabinet a draft of a proposed foreign policy statement incorporating the positions they had already discussed. Because Canning's original proposal had been made confidentially and provided no apparent public basis for such a statement of policy, Monroe felt that he required some obvious reason for declaring America's resolutions regarding Europe and the Western Hemisphere. When the Russian minister, Baron de Tuyll, sent Adams a note to inform him that the tsar of Russia hoped the revolutions in Latin America would fail, it gave Monroe a sufficient reason to declare publicly U.S. policy. Monroe instructed Adams to prepare a statement to present to Canning that would officially reject the notion of a joint resolution but inform the British that the United States agreed in principle with their views opposing European intervention in Latin America.

By this time, Monroe had decided to go beyond Adams's notion that the whole matter should be handled through diplomatic correspondence alone. Monroe had been working on his annual message, to be delivered on December 2, and he added to his message the elements developed in concert with the Cabinet. Thus did the president make public in reasonably dramatic form the feelings of his administration regarding the Western Hemisphere, feelings that he believed most Americans shared.

In his address Monroe made four points that came to make up the Monroe Doctrine. He asserted the unique character of the American political system in opposition to the old European systems. He declared that the American continents (that is, the Western Hemisphere) were no longer to be colonized by any European country. The United States would consider any such attempt at colonization or any attempt to install a European political agenda a danger to the security and welfare of the region. Finally, the United States would not interfere in European politics nor in the affairs of existing European colonies.

As a tough, unilateral statement, a warning to the great powers, the collection of paragraphs interspersed through the annual message had the immediate impact Monroe sought. He did not believe the United States alone could prevent further interference in the Americas; he merely wanted to clarify the stance of the U.S. government so that no mistakes would occur through ignorance of the American position. He knew, as did Canning and others, that Britain's navy was the real impediment to European interference in American affairs. What Monroe's words did was to provide satisfaction to the American public, a sense of national self-worth, as well as to ally the United States publicly with the aspirations of the Latin American independence movements.

Monroe did not conceive that he was in the process of promulgating a "doctrine" that would become one of the cornerstones of future U.S. policy. The very term "doctrine" would not come into vogue until the mid-19th century. During the 1840s, James Polk would be the first president to make an issue of the "Monroe Doctrine." Thereafter, it would be appealed to only infrequently throughout most of the remainder of the century.

> *The American continents, by the free and independent condition which they have assumed and maintain, are henceforth not to be considered as the subjects for future colonization by any European powers.*
> —JAMES MONROE

President Monroe outlines the provisions of the Monroe Doctrine to the members of his cabinet. The doctrine's policy against U.S. involvement in European wars was violated by the United States with its entrance into World War I.

Nor did Monroe intend to fling out to the world a declaration of American imperialism. The statements made on December 2, 1823, were not prepared to lay the groundwork for extensive American colonization or intervention throughout the hemisphere or to enforce the spread of the American political system to other parts of the Americas. True, Monroe had warned Europeans not to seek to extend their systems to the Western Hemisphere, but he had confidence that republicanism, on its own merits, would inevitably replace despotism in all corners of the world. He was content to have a strong American republic, recognized and respected. So long as Latin America was not threatened by the great powers of Europe, it could develop at its own pace.

Reception of the message varied. Americans generally approved, finding in Monroe's words ample cause for national pride. But if Monroe hoped that his declarations would establish the United States as the prime defender of independence in the eyes of Latin Americans, he was not to be rewarded. Though a few expressed some appreciation, most of them accepted the fact that the British fleet had more to say on the matter than the president of the United States. And as though to prove that the United States had little to offer, when the new nation of Colombia ventured to ask for a military alliance with the United States in 1824, Monroe politely turned them down, claiming there was no danger of interference from Europe that warranted it. The British press mainly welcomed the American position as commensurate with British objectives, but Canning was quick to contend that the noncolonization clause set forth by Monroe could not be considered binding on Britain.

A long-standing trade war with Britain over American access to the British West Indies seemed to make Monroe's "doctrine" a pointed reaction more to Britain than to France, Spain, or Russia. Resolution of the trade impasse had to wait until Andrew Jackson's presidency in the 1830s, and the British would ignore Monroe's hemispheric claims for a far longer time, continuing to interfere in the Americas.

As 1824 waned, Monroe reached the final days of his two terms as president. William Crawford, partially paralyzed by a stroke, received the Republican caucus's selection as the party's official candidate, but few Republicans bothered to attend the caucus, which had outlived its attractiveness. Other means were being used to nominate contenders. State legislatures sponsored candidates, and the party "convention," at least at the state level, had made its appearance. Not just Crawford but Henry Clay, Andrew Jackson, and John Quincy Adams sought to be Monroe's successor. Monroe kept his preference to himself.

The outgoing president was anxious to depart. Like Jefferson, he had been in office long enough to perceive his initial popularity give way in the face of carping criticism and genuine dislike. New men were eager to get on with power brokering, and the elderly gentleman in the White House, in his old-fashioned clothes, had become an anachronism. Virginia beckoned.

Our respectability abroad and prosperity at home are the best eulogy of his administration.
—Toast to Monroe at a dinner in his honor, 1824

8

In Search of Vindication

Monroe retreated from public office to Oak Hill, his estate near Richmond, Virginia, where he hoped to live out his life in familiar and agreeable surroundings and to care for his wife, who had been in ill health for a long time. Like his predecessors, he chose not to interfere further in national political life. Jefferson's death in 1826 deprived him of a close confidante, but the void was filled by Monroe's now closer relationship with Madison. Monroe became a member of the Board of Visitors of Jefferson's beloved University of Virginia in Charlottesville, where, following Jefferson's death, Madison became rector.

The aging Monroe tried his hand at political philosophy, at which Jefferson and Madison had excelled. He began work on a treatise, the shortened title of which was *The People the Sovereigns*, but stopped writing it in 1829, and it remained unfinished at his death. Chosen, along with Madison, to be an elector from Virginia for presidential candidate John Quincy Adams in 1828, he joined his Republican colleague in turning down the honor.

> *It was with a sense of relief that Monroe turned over the reins of power to Adams on March 4, 1825.*
> —HARRY AMMON
> Monroe biographer

Monroe's second term as president expired in 1825. The elderly Virginian relinquished the office with a certain degree of bitterness over what he believed was a lack of recognition of his achievements as chief executive.

In 1825 Monroe retired to Oak Hill, his country estate in Loudoun County, Virginia. The affluent trappings of Oak Hill belied the true, debt-ridden state of Monroe's financial affairs.

Throughout his retirement, Monroe battled with two of his old adversaries: financial need and deep concern for his reputation. Never as financially well off as his colleagues, Monroe had spent a lifetime grappling with debts and trying to make ends meet. Not his lands nor the infrequent practice of the law nor salary in public office had provided income enough to cover the expenses of family and career, and he was forced now to find means to pay off a $75,000 debt. He owed money both to banks and friends, and he could not count on earning enough from his estates or vocation to pay his debts. He tried to sell Highland but could not even get its appraised value, so he sold off some of the land to reduce his debt with the federal bank.

Added to his financial concerns, Monroe had a desperate urge to achieve personal vindication and wanted recognition for his years of service to the nation and for the achievements he held to be his. Too often he had had to explain his actions, defend his conduct, confront his critics. His two great diplomatic missions had ended in seeming failure:

Washington had recalled him from France in 1796 in virtual disgrace, and Jefferson and Madison had rejected the Monroe-Pinkney draft treaty in 1806, the prime achievement of his several years in Paris, Madrid, and London. His candidacy against Madison in 1808 had likewise been an embarrassment. His presidency, which had started with "good feelings," had ended in bitter intraparty strife (the Republicans were splitting into Calhoun and Jackson camps) and the widely shared sense that Monroe, one of the last leaders of the generation that had been shaped by the revolutionary war, had outlived his usefulness.

The battleground Monroe chose to campaign on, both to recoup his personal fortune and restore his political honor, involved claims against the U.S. government for monies owed him for past services.

The bed to which Elizabeth Monroe was frequently confined during the years that followed her husband's retirement. Monroe tended faithfully to his invalid wife until her death in September 1830.

Chief Justice John Marshall, Monroe's old friend and fellow revolutionary. Marshall and Monroe were elected to Virginia's constitutional convention in 1829. Monroe, preoccupied with his wife's failing health and the poor state of his financial affairs, took little part in the debates.

Monroe felt that payment of the money owed him would not only help his financial situation but would constitute a recognition of distinguished service to the country. Even before he had left office, Monroe had requested of Congress that the Treasury pay him for out-of-pocket expenses he had accrued as a diplomat in his early career. Over the next five years, the amount of money he requested would escalate and the nature of his claims expand as he and Congress scuffled back and forth, haggling over responsibilities and dollars. Increasingly haunting the process for Congress was the specter of an ex-president, ill and old, on the threshold of poverty.

In early January 1825, Monroe asked Congress both to investigate any alleged improprieties connected with his administration and at the same time to consider whether outstanding payments were due him for past services. He submitted memoirs to a select committee of the House of Representatives, the first of which detailed his diplomatic accounts since 1794, the second explaining his innocence in a matter involving misappropriation of government funds intended for the restoration of the White House after the War of 1812. Congress, not wanting to pursue Monroe, accepted his explanation about the funds, and ended the investigation. Monroe, feeling he had had a chance to explain himself, also let the matter drop.

He kept alive, however, the issue of monies he believed himself entitled to. As early as 1816, as incumbent president, Monroe had pressed various claims arising from his missions to Europe in 1794 and 1803, and he had been reimbursed. Now he submitted a new list of demands having to do with salaries and living expenditures while a U.S. envoy. Monroe wanted $53,000. In 1826 a House committee trimmed the more extravagant charges and recommended a figure of $29,513. The House, however, cut it even further to $15,900. The Senate pressured the House to restore the full $29,513, and President Adams signed the bill. Monroe took the money, but he was still in difficulties. He sadly turned over most of the Highland property to the Bank of the United States to pay off a $25,000 debt.

Because critics were contending that he had already received too much money from the government, in November 1826 he wrote a defense of his claims, *The Memoir of James Monroe, Esq., relating to his Unsettled Claims upon the People and Government of the United States*, which appeared in the *National Intelligencer*. Monroe's hopes for additional compensation had to wait until the 1828 election was decided. He ran into trouble with Jackson when a report misleadingly implied that he had not supported the general during the 1818 Florida crisis. When Monroe was then chosen as an elector for Jackson's opponent, John Quincy Adams (even though he declined), the Jackson camp became openly hostile. When Jackson then won the election, all this seemed to doom Monroe's hopes for further compensation through Congress.

In October 1829, Monroe performed a final public service at a convention called in Richmond to restructure the state's constitution. There Monroe worked for the last time with a group of fellow Virginians, including Madison, John Marshall (chief justice of the Supreme Court and his old comrade from the revolutionary war), John Randolph, and the governor of Virginia, William Branch Giles. During the sessions Monroe urged moderation on issues that threatened the state with sectional division. Growing infirmity led him to withdraw from the deliberations by the end of the year.

That same year, the citizens of Albemarle County, Virginia, petitioned Congress in Monroe's behalf. They stated that Monroe had surrendered his chances for gaining personal wealth through private ventures by devoting many years of his life to public service. Another House committee, chaired by a friend of Monroe's from Ablemarle County, reviewed the request and recommended that an additional $60,000 be awarded him. The track of the petition then grew increasingly more circuitous.

A portrait of the 82-year-old James Madison wearing a sleeping cap. When Thomas Jefferson died in 1826, Madison and Monroe once more renewed their friendship. The two former presidents — whose relationship had seen many ups and downs — remained close through their waning years.

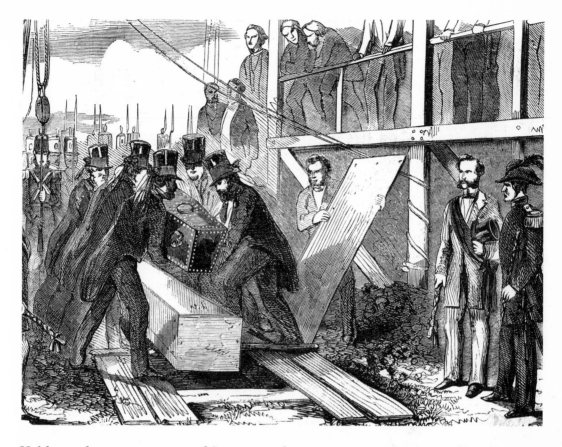

Held over for a new session of Congress, the petition was put aside when the long-simmering storm between Jackson and Calhoun erupted. Finally, after much lobbying in Monroe's favor, a compromise emerged, and in February 1831, the House granted him $30,000.

In both senses in which he had sought restitution, Monroe had to have been disappointed. In all he got $68,500, which he must have compared to the $200,000 Congress had voted in 1824 for the Marquis de Lafayette for services rendered during the American Revolution; Lafayette also received an enormous tract of land. Moreover, Monroe considered all opposition to the full payment of his claims as a personal attack on his honor and service. He even had to suffer by innuendo the charge that he had been overpaid when he felt that he had been grossly slighted.

Following an elaborate state funeral, James Monroe's remains are lowered into the ground at Holywood Cemetery in Richmond, Virginia. Monroe died in New York City on the Fourth of July, 1831.

The news of the compensation in 1831 came too late for Monroe to derive any real satisfaction from it, for he had suffered personal tragedies in the fall of 1830 that had devastated him. On September 21, his son-in-law and longtime supporter, George Hay, died. Two days later, Monroe's beloved wife died. Beset by failing health since he had fallen from a horse in 1828 and distraught by his wife's death, Monroe went to New York City to live with his daughter Maria Hester and her husband, Samuel Gouverneur, the city's postmaster.

In April 1831, Monroe resigned from the University of Virginia's Board of Visitors in a letter to Madison in which Monroe wrote that his greatest regret was that he would never see his dear friend again. On July 4, 1831 — the 55th anniversary of the Revolution — James Monroe died in New York City. As had Jefferson and John Adams, who both had died on July 4, 1826, he died at a symbolic moment. He received a lavish funeral in New York, and his body was borne in procession to the Gouverneur vault, where he was buried. Days of mourning were declared throughout the nation for one of the last of those great men of the Revolution, who had made the country a nation.

Monroe had conveyed a dual vision to that nation he had helped to launch. On the one hand, he was among the earliest to understand and favor westward growth, to listen to and address the needs of the pioneers who crossed the mountains into the heartland of America. On the other hand, he had looked eastward toward Europe and imagined a day when the United States would be regarded as an important power in world politics. If the "doctrine" he had stated in 1823 was slightly premature, little matter. His beloved nation had survived and was growing.

In 1858, Monroe's remains, carefully lifted from his burying place in New York City, were reverently returned to Virginia soil. Native son, governor, statesman, the last of the imposing Virginia dynasty of presidents, Monroe had come home for the last time, his public service completed, his memory honored.

JAMES MONROE
1758-1831

Perhaps to a greater degree than any of his contemporaries, James Monroe recognized the potential of the United States for an almost unlimited growth, and, although he lacked Jefferson's charisma and Madison's political insight, his contribution to the young nation was as significant as theirs.

Further Reading

Ammon, Harry. *James Monroe: The Quest for National Identity.* New York: McGraw-Hill, 1971.

Bruns, Roger. *George Washington.* New York: Chelsea House, 1987.

———. *Thomas Jefferson.* New York: Chelsea House, 1987.

Dangerfield, George. *The Awakening of American Nationalism, 1815–1828.* New York: Harper & Row, 1965.

———. *The Era of Good Feelings.* New York: Harcourt, Brace & World, 1952.

DuVal, Miles P. *James Monroe: An Appreciation. Highlights of his Life and the Monroe Doctrine.* Orange, VA: James Monroe Memorial Foundation, 1982.

May, Ernest R. *The Making of the Monroe Doctrine.* Cambridge, MA: Harvard University Press, 1975.

Monroe, James. *The Autobiography of James Monroe.* Syracuse, NY: Syracuse University Press, 1959.

Morgan, George. *The Life of James Monroe.* New York: AMS Press, 1969.

O'Brien, Steven. *Alexander Hamilton.* New York: Chelsea House, 1989.

Perkins, Dexter. *The Monroe Doctrine: 1823–1826.* Gloucester, MA: P. Smith, 1965.

Smelser, Marshall. *The Democratic Republic: 1801–1815.* New York: Harper & Row, 1968.

Vaughan, Harold Cecil. *The Monroe Doctrine, 1823: A Landmark in American Foreign Policy.* New York: Watts, 1973.

Wilmerding, Lucius Jr. *James Monroe, Public Claimant.* New Bruswick, NJ: Rutgers University Press, 1960.

Chronology

April 28, 1758	Born James Monroe in Westmoreland County, Virginia
1774	Enters William and Mary College
1776	War of Independence begins
1776–78	Monroe sees action in the battles of New York, Trenton, Brandywine, Germantown, and Monmouth
1780–82	Studies law in Virginia as protégé of Governor Thomas Jefferson
1782	Elected to Virginia House of Delegates and Governor's Council
1783	War of Independence ends
1783–86	Monroe serves as a member of Virginia delegation in Congress
1787	U.S. Constitution drafted in Philadelphia
1788	Monroe serves as a delegate to Virginia Ratifying Convention
1789	George Washington becomes first president; French Revolution begins
1790	Monroe elected U.S. senator from Virginia
1794–96	Serves as U.S. minister to France
1796	John Adams elected president
1799–1802	Monroe serves as governor of Virginia
1800	Helps quell Gabriel's slave uprising; Thomas Jefferson elected president
1803	Monroe appointed envoy extraordinary to France; helps Robert Livingston secure Louisiana Purchase
1803–1806	Serves as U.S. minister to Great Britain
1806	Drafts Monroe-Pinkney Treaty with Thomas Pinkney
1807	U.S. warship *Chesapeake* fired on by British
1808	Madison elected president, defeating Monroe
1811–17	Monroe serves as secretary of state and acting secretary of war
1812	U.S. declares war on Great Britain
1814	Monroe helps in defense of Washington and Baltimore
1815	Treaty of Ghent ends war
1816	Monroe elected president
1817	Makes Era of Good Feelings tour
1820	Accepts Missouri Compromise legislation; is reelected president; receives all but one electoral vote
1823	Presents Monroe Doctrine address to Congress
1824	John Quincy Adams elected president
1825–31	Monroe battles Congress for payment of personal claims
1828	Injured in fall from horse; Andrew Jackson elected president
1829	Monroe serves as delegate to Virginia Constitutional Convention
1830	Moves to New York City to live with daughter following wife's death
July 4, 1831	Dies in New York City

Index

Charles Wetzel is a professor of history at Drew University, where he teaches early American social and intellectual history. He holds a Ph.D. from the University of Wisconsin, where he was President Adams Fellow in American History. He has also taught at the State University of New York and Purdue University. His scholarly publications have focused on American philanthropy and on refugees in American intellectual life. In his spare moments he writes poetry and fiction and spends time with his family.

Arthur M. Schlesinger, jr., taught history at Harvard for many years and is currently Albert Schweitzer Professor of the Humanities at City University of New York. He is the author of numerous highly praised works in American history and has twice been awarded the Pulitzer Prize. He served in the White House as special assistant to Presidents Kennedy and Johnson.
